Overcoming Fe

A practical guide for women who overanalyze,

overthink, and are overly analytical

Kiran Bedi

Get a free mini workbook at:

http://eepurl.com/gimJRH

For any questions or suggestions, email the author at:

GSFProductions@ctemplar.com

Dedication

To my dad, my biggest champion.

And to all the women who overanalyze.

I see you. I am one of you.

We are in this together.

Disclaimer

Disclaimer #1: This book aims to provide information and motivation to the readers; the content is the sole expression and opinion of the author. The author does not intend to render any type of psychological, legal, or any other kind of professional advice to the readers.

Disclaimer #2: The author takes no responsibility for any physical, psychological, emotional, financial, or commercial damages, including, but not limited to, special, incidental, consequential, or other damages.

Disclaimer #3: The tools presented and described in the book require consistent practice, discipline, and commitment. The tools shared in the book show results if you work toward making these suggestions a part of your life.

Why Did I Write This Book?

First and foremost, I feel incredibly honored and excited that you are reading this book. My intention for this book is to offer advice that would help you in overcoming any fears or failures that might stop you from taking action and becoming the best version of yourself.

As someone who overanalyzes, overthinks, and is obsessively analytical, I've lived a logical, sensible, and rational life. Most important decisions of my life were "carefully" thought through. But fear ruled my life and limited my choices as I didn't want to fail in my endeavors. Looking back, I can confidently say I had lived an extremely dull life.

Education was the number-one priority in my home growing up. Thus, academia was a breeze for me. I was an A+ student throughout my days at school and college, and I had no concept of failure. My philosophy during school and college was: "Hard work is the key to success. You work hard, you achieve success. Period."

My mindset drastically changed when I stepped outside the closed walls of academia. The world outside turned out to be a very different experience, one I was utterly unprepared for.

I experienced failure in almost every aspect of my life—in personal relationships, at work, in starting a company, buying my first house.

And the list goes on. With each failure came a litany of irrational fears. And these fears simply refused to leave.

I could no longer "work hard" my way into success. In fact, my mindset of "working hard" backfired on more occasions than I can count. However, I had managed to pull myself together because, after all, "Hard work is the key to success," right?

And then, the year 2014 came along.

I had just started to learn about stock trading, spending considerable amounts of time studying the financial markets and analyzing the next best move, and yet, when it came time to pull the trigger, I would hesitate. All sorts of fears would start looming in my head.

Every day, it was the same darn story—I did the analysis, then fears started swirling in my head, so I didn't pull the trigger.

During this time, I felt extreme levels of fear; their intensity felt off the charts. I had never felt fear to that degree ever in my life.

Every day was an emotional roller-coaster ride, followed by intense fear. I was shocked, intrigued, and fascinated by my emotional swings. I had never seen anyone experience such fear.

I would ask myself questions like:

- Why in the world won't I pull the darn switch (as in buy or sell stocks per my analysis)?
- Why am I afraid to lose?
- So what if I fail? It's not the end of the world!

From an intellectual perspective, I understood that fear and failure are a stepping stone to success, and yet I lacked the skills and the mindset to put it into practice. Besides, the perfectionist streak in me didn't make things any easier.

You know how some people feel the fear and get over it in the next second? God bless these folks! Sadly, I wasn't like them. I felt all the irrational fears intensely, and, unfortunately, I just couldn't get over them in the blink of an eye.

However, I vowed to help myself and address the root cause of these roller-coaster emotional swings. Since I had never experienced fear to such an intensity before, there was nothing in my intellectual mind that I could draw upon.

So, I set upon exploring various tools and modalities, reading books, and attending retreats and workshops that resonated with me. Nothing was off limits. If I felt any book/retreat/research had a remote chance of helping me soothe my untamed emotions—I went all in.

The tools I explored and embraced helped me experience noticeable shifts and success in dealing with and dissolving the fear patterns.

Through persistence, I had finally managed to get a handle on fear. I finally got what fear and failure felt like in my body; more importantly, I knew what to do about it.

This book includes the list of tools that helped me dismantle the invisible walls of self-sabotage induced by fear. I hope that these tools will help you as well to gain the needed momentum toward completing your projects and achieving your dreams.

Creating a "fearless" mindset seemed like walking on a less traveled road. The journey felt bumpy, perilous, and crooked, with tiny peaks and deep valleys. Then again, had my analytical mind known upfront what the journey would be like, it would have never signed up for it.

There are still moments when I feel that intense fear, and that's when I return to the tools that I will be sharing with you in this book. Through consistent use of these tools, I have experienced a substantial shift in my ability to handle fears and failures.

Who Is This Book For?

Are you someone who likes to "figure things out" before stepping forward? Do you prefer to foresee and plan for every potential pitfall that you could encounter in your new endeavors? Someone who loves to slice and dice new ideas from every angle to see whether they make any "logical" sense or not? Do you want to start your own business, but your fear of failure (or even success) is holding you back? Or maybe you're someone who wants to experience this big and beautiful world, but you remain too afraid to relinquish your fat paycheck?

Whichever one you are, and if fear is stopping you from becoming the best you can be, then this book is for you!

Don't worry, all of us have our own fears to various degrees. But here's an interesting fact: ***Only a small fraction of our fears are rational. The majority of our fears are completely irrational.***

Women who overanalyze, like me and perhaps like you, usually have fears that look like this:
- Fear of being imperfect.
- Fear of being a failure.
- Fear of being wrong.
- Fear of making mistakes.
- Fear of being broke (even if they are earning a six-figure salary).
- Fear of the unknown.

- Fear of losing control.
- Fear of being bored.
- Fear of lack of safety.
- Fear of death.

If you can identify with any of these fears, then I have wonderful news to share—you are not alone!

I was in your shoes, not too long ago. When fear controls your mind, it stops you on a consistent basis, bringing forth frustration and even outright depression.

And so, I hope that the tools I will share in this book are going to help you get unstuck and gain momentum towards the projects, dreams, and goals that mean the world to you.

You will see a lot of different ideas suggested in this book, but I urge you—please!—only follow what resonates with you, personally, and ignore the rest. All of us are unique in our own right, so look for tools that complement your uniqueness.

I know your time is extremely valuable to you; hence, I have purposefully kept this book short and concise.

Thanks for your time and happy reading.

Table of Contents

Section 1: Introduction..14

    Chapter 1 — Fear as a Full Body Experience 15

Section 2: Removing Fear From the Mental Body..................................26

    Chapter 2 — Identifying Fear-based Patterns in the Mental Body 27

    Chapter 3 — Common Blocks in an "Overly Analytical" Mental Body
....38

    Chapter 4 — Tools for the Mental Body Reset...................................65

Section 3: Removing Fear From the Emotional Body.............................93

    Chapter 5 — Getting to Know the Emotional Body...........................94

    Chapter 6 — Fear and Its Other Emotional Friends 98

    Chapter 7 — Tools for the Emotional Body Reset...........................101

Section 4: Removing Fear From the Physical Body 133

    Chapter 8 — Your Body's Reaction to Fear 134

    Chapter 9 — Your Brain on Fear..137

    Chapter 10 — Tools for the Physical Body Reset 145

Section 5: Becoming an "Actionist" in the Face of Fear 171

    Chapter 11 — Tools to Counter Potential Pitfalls 172

What's Possible When We Do the Inner Emotional Work 176

Acknowledgments...179

Additional Resources...181

Bonus Material 183

About Kiran Bedi 184

Section 1: Introduction

Chapter 1 — Fear as a Full Body Experience

As I mentioned before, some years back, I dabbled in the stock market. I spent hours looking at the data, analyzing it, and identifying patterns for understanding, and they would often lead to good conclusions. I was confident. I was ready!

But then I would start feeling fear. Awful, powerful fear that exceeded anything I had ever felt before, or even heard of, stopping me from taking action. Every day I would do this: figure out the best outcome, then fail to act because of that wretched fear. Whenever a wave of fear washed over me, I felt a sense of dread in my body; I would enter a state of panic and anxiety that made my mind blank out.

Back then, I didn't know how to deal with these overwhelming feelings of panic, fear, and anxiety. What helped during that time was going for long walks in nature. These long walks would instantly put my body at ease and lift the weight my intense feelings were bringing. Spending time in nature rejuvenated my body, mind, and spirit. It was my go-to tool in times of emotional unease. But the moment I went back to my trading desk, those intense feelings would return with full force. This cycle of emotional distress lasted for many months.

To overcome the emotional anguish I was experiencing, I tried many juvenile tactics. Firstly, I tried hiding my emotions and running away from them, pretending they weren't there. Then I tried to convince myself that the anxiety and fear would magically disappear, if only I showed perseverance! Obviously, none of these tactics worked. No matter what I did, the intensity of these emotions would just not diminish.

When "everything" failed, I decided to take a break from trading and find a way to help myself from the continual onslaught of emotional overwhelm and stress.

And so, for the next few months, I spent a lot of time in meditation, praying for guidance. I also worked closely with a chiropractor to help me deal with these challenging emotions, and I kept a journal of my experiences.

Then, one day, while I was journaling, it dawned on me that my emotional distress was affecting:
- My body (through my physical sensations).
- My mind (through my thinking).
- My emotional state (through my feelings).

This was an eye-opener for me because *I had never imagined fear existed as a "full body experience," as in: fear could affect my body and mind (besides my emotions)*.

Until this moment, I naively rationalized that if I could change all my "negative" thoughts into "positive" ones, then all my "bad" feelings of panic, fear, and anxiety would disappear.

I realized that I had to look beyond the "think positive and think happy" mindset to heal the emotional suffering.

I started looking for solutions that addressed the body, mind, and emotions as a collective unit, rather than focusing on the mindset alone.

The "Four Bodies Model"

In 2016, I enrolled for an online meditation course. One of the introductory courses included the "Four Bodies Model" that described the human energy systems. According to this model, the human body is comprised of four distinct layers:

1. Physical Body.
2. Emotional Body.
3. Mental Body.
4. Spiritual Body.

The **Physical Body** is the body you see when you look in the mirror. You experience your life through your body. At the physical level, matter vibrates at its most dense level and appears solid.

The **Emotional Body** is the sum of all your emotional experiences. This body allows you to feel and reciprocate emotions like love, joy, anger, sadness, and tenderness, among others. Your Emotional Body occupies the same space as the Physical Body but vibrates at a higher frequency.

The **Mental Body** houses the "ego mind" and the "divine mind." This body lets you think and analyze. The educational system focuses on developing the Mental Body and rewards the accomplishments of your intellectual mind.

The **Spiritual Body** houses higher vibrational states of expanded awareness, enlightenment, awakening, and mystical self.

Here is a visual of the Four Bodies Model.

Four Bodies Model

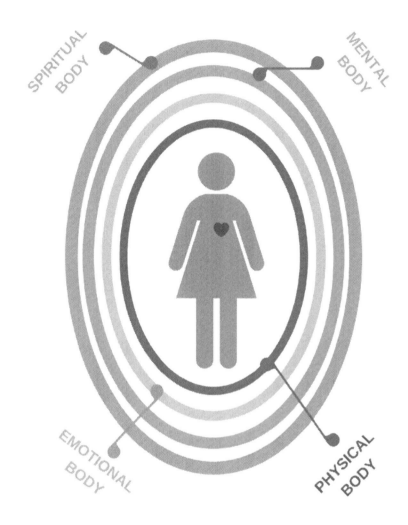

As I contemplated the Four Bodies Model, it dawned on me that when I feel fear, a fear response gets triggered in my body.

A response to fear affects my:

- Mental Body (through my thinking).

- Emotional Body (through my feelings).
- Physical Body (through my physical sensations, like panic-induced sweating).
- Spiritual Body.

I realized that emotional distress affected both the mind and the body in a very negative way. I needed to fix it, to change it, and my contemplation of the Four Bodies Model fortified my understanding of emotional distress, allowing me to find ways to heal it.

This led me to conclude that when a person feels fear, then fear affects all four layers of the human body.

And if this hypothesis was true, I needed to heal the fear-based emotions from all four layers of the body. That is, I need to alter the:
- Fear-based Physical responses (coming from the Physical Body).
- Fear-based Emotional responses (coming from the Emotional Body).
- Fear-based Mental responses (coming from the Mental Body).
- Fear-based Spiritual responses (coming from the Spiritual Body).

And so, for the next two years, that is precisely what I worked toward.
I explored healing fear responses at the physical, mental, and emotional level.

We know that the body and the mind function as one unit. We cannot determine where the mind ends and the body starts, and vice versa. And yet the hypothesis that the fear had to be healed from all four layers of the body gave my overanalytical mind a modicum of control over exploring and researching tools to overcoming it.

Through countless trial-and-error attempts, I had finally understood the frequency of fear, what it looked like, and, more importantly, how to overcome it. I have since uncovered many tools that have helped me to relieve myself of the old fear patterns, and I will share the most potent tools with you in this book.

By no means does this book contain every tool one can find for emotional, mental, or physical healing; these are just the ones that I have experienced as successful. Again, and I can't stress this enough, please only take what resonates with you, and only you, and ignore the rest. I suggest that you filter all information through your heart resonance. So, let's get started.

What Makes Adults Emotionally Healthy?

To effectively and permanently overcome fear, you need to address and heal the "fear responses" from all the four layers of your body. When the four layers (or the four bodies) work in harmony with each other, you feel balanced, peaceful, and ready to voyage into the unknown.

Having equally developed four layers of our bodies makes adults emotionally healthy and balanced.

When the four layers are not working in perfect synchronization, the negative outcome manifests as dissonance in the body. The disconnect between what you think, what you feel, and what you truly desire is blatantly evident and can be agonizing. This internal agitation and lack of synchronization causes you to feel intense fear in your body. So, to overcome the fear of failure and failure itself, you must address all four bodies—Mental, Physical, Emotional, and Spiritual—and have them work in unison.

When all four bodies work in harmony, the constant low frequencies of fear or anxiety over failure can no longer harass you.

To develop all four bodies, you must remove the fear from each layer. In the next three sections, we will explore tools that will assist you in alleviating the fear responses in your Mental Body, Emotional Body, and Physical Body.

Overdeveloped Mental Bodies of Women Who Overthink

When you tend to overthink or overanalyze, it is an indication that the four bodies are not working in synchronization and may be unequally developed.

In most overthinkers:

- **The Mental Body is overdeveloped and overidentified with**. In other words, overthinkers prefer to *think* about situations instead of *feeling* them.
- **The Mental Body tends to overcompensate for the less-developed Emotional Body.**
- The psychological perspective tells us that the Mental Body is compensating for the less-developed Emotional Body by suffering and enduring. This manifests in terms of "sucking it up," "putting on a brave face," withholding communication, working through exhaustion, living in denial, etc.
- The Physical Body lacks the vitality and flexibility seen in emotionally healthy adults because excessive energy is expended on intellectual pursuits.

Do you identify as an overthinker based on the description here?

Discovering Your Emotional Age

Emotionally charged experiences from childhood, and even adulthood, can stunt the natural growth and evolution of the Emotional Body. Trauma can freeze the energy in all four layers of your body. People who have undergone severe trauma usually rely on coping mechanisms, which only mask but do not heal the problems, to deal with the challenges of daily life.

It won't be an exaggeration to say that someone who has undergone trauma or intense emotional experiences may have a biological age of, say, 30 years and the mental age of, say, 25 years, but remain an infant in their emotional maturity.

When you think of maturity of your Physical Body, Mental Body, and Emotional Body, what age number comes to your mind?
- Are your Mental Body, Emotional Body, and Physical Body of the same age?
- If not, which body feels the oldest to you?
- Which body feels underdeveloped to you?

From this simple exercise, can you identify which body needs most of your attention?

When I started tending to my emotions, I realized that I trusted my intellect far more than my feelings. Outwardly, this manifested as a conflict between my head and heart. When my heart nudged me to do something, I would do everything but that.

Clearly, while my Mental Body had free reign in its expression and exploration, my Emotional Body's freedom was non-existent. I didn't realize that I had imprisoned my Emotional Body by denying my own feelings.

The more I gave myself permission to feel a full range of emotions, the more I was able to liberate my Emotional Body from my self-inflicted imprisonment. Eventually, my Emotional Body caught up to my Mental Body in growth, freedom, and expression.

As you clear the fear responses from your Emotional, Mental, Physical, and Spiritual layers, you will experience a greater harmony and synchronization between the Four Bodies. This is because you eventually stop overidentifying with one or more bodies. And, as you become internally harmonious, you cannot help but become a healthy and emotionally balanced individual. That makes overcoming fear of anything easy, literally like a walk in the park.

Please note that discussion on the Spiritual Body has been intentionally excluded from this book.

Section 2: Removing Fear From the Mental Body

Chapter 2 — Identifying Fear-based Patterns in the Mental Body

To break the bondage loop of fear, you must acknowledge your fears. More often than not, fear doesn't show up as fear itself; rather, **fear disguises itself as resistance**.

Consider a scenario: you have started your own company and successfully launched it into the business world. You are now planning on taking your business to the next level, maybe grow it from a five to a six-figure income.

To make this jump, you make a list of things you need to do. Let's imagine that your list to turn that into reality looks like this: putting yourself or your brand on YouTube, speaking at events, engaging the influencing figures in your industry, marketing, and advertising your business to new clients through various means; that's all you need.

Now you know what tasks to complete. And yet you hold yourself back from taking massive actions in the outer world. Why?

You don't put yourself on social media platforms (perhaps under the pretense that you're shy). You shy away from speaking at business gatherings or turn down invitations entirely. You don't market yourself to businesses or potential customers. You know which steps to take, and still, you find yourself procrastinating.

This is the resistance I am talking about. You know what actions to take, but you won't do them. Sound familiar?

Resistance can show up in many areas of life. Some areas are blatantly obvious, while others are not so much. When multiple areas of your life overlap, it becomes challenging to discern what exactly you are resisting, and the underlying cause of resistance (fear) is often not self-evident.

Resistance can also show up as conflicting thoughts in your head that look like this:
- Should I do this, or should I stay away?
- I want to explore new avenues, but I don't know if I can handle them.
- I don't know if this job/partner/business/idea/house is "the one."

These conflicting thoughts spiral downward into exhausting and repetitive mental loops. When you find yourself confused or overwhelmed with conflicting beliefs and ideas, find a way to connect with your heart.

Start by asking yourself these questions every single day:
- What does my heart yearn for?
- What brings me the most joy?
- What am I most unsatisfied with in my life?
- Which unfulfilled dreams does my heart keep coming back to?

Your heart will always nudge you toward your greater destiny. When you silence your busy mind and tune into the vibrations of your heart, you will find the answers you seek.

As an example, I always yearned to write a book. In fact, I have been desiring to write a book for years. While my mind exploded with creative ideas, I would resist writing under the pretense of having too many topics to choose from. Sounds silly, I know, and, that is how I resisted writing.

In retrospect, I can see that the root cause of this resistance was fear. However, at that time, I lacked that clarity.

So, to rephrase, I was resisting:

Writing a book.

Now, it's your turn for this exercise.

Once you have clarity, write down the top three areas in which you are resisting change:

1. _____
2. _____
3. _____

If you feel obstructed for any reason, don't let your busy mind fool you. Ask your heart for guidance to reveal areas that have been long denied growth and change by your fears.

Fear and Its Faithful Sidekick—Failure

I like to think of failure as a sidekick of fear. Fear and failure almost always go hand-in-hand. When fear isn't the root cause of resistance, then it's almost always a failure, and vice versa.

Consider a scenario: your boss has nominated you for your company's annual public speaking event. Let's assume that public speaking is not your forte. Your palms start to sweat, and your heart begins to race at the very thought of public speaking. You can't imagine speaking to top managers at your firm, be there 20 or 200 of them.

You may think to yourself, "What if I ruin my presentation by stuttering or something? What if no one understands what I'm saying? What if I get poor and negative feedback, or worse—what if I get no feedback? What if my voice shakes? What if I make a fool of myself?"

If you look closely, all the "what-if" scenarios represent some form of possible failure. This is fear, only disguised as failure.

In the thick of emotions, you tend to form what-if scenarios in your head, rather than acknowledging that you are experiencing the fear of failure, or fear of success, and so on and so forth. Earlier, I shared with you that I wanted to write a book but kept resisting that notion. I would open my notebook and just stare at the blank pages, taking no action whatsoever.

Instead of forming sentences of my writing, my mind would play out all the what-if scenarios, in a constant loop. My reasoning included thoughts like:

- What if I can't write beyond 10 pages?
- What if I have nothing of value to share?
- What if I waste someone's time?
- What if my book is not good enough?
- What if I get zero sales?

After a considerable time, it dawned on me that the what-if scenarios were merely a mask for my deep-seated fears.

When I started paying close attention to my what-if list, I realized that I could synthesize all the what-ifs into two main core fears:

- Fear of being judged.
- Fear of being a failure.

Consequently, when I connected my what-ifs with my core fears, my list looked like this:

What-if Scenarios/Failures	Core Fears
- What if I got zero sales? - What if my book doesn't help anyone? - What if I suck at writing?	- Fear of being judged
- What if I can't write beyond 10 pages? - What if I have nothing of value to share? - What if I waste someone's time? - What if my book is not good enough?	- Fear of being a failure

I had never written a book in my entire life, and I didn't know what it took to write, much less publish a book. And I certainly had no way of predicting the outcome of my actions.

The possibility of an impending failure scared my perfectionist streak to no end. I mean, it was a big deal! After all, I had spent all my life avoiding failure. There was no way my analytical mind would embrace the thought of a potential failure.

However, I found a way to work around this sticky problem. Before I share the secret, please complete this exercise on identifying your core fears. It's important that all of your core fears are properly identified before you can proceed to the point of healing them.

As you work through the exercise, some of the fears and the reasoning might sound silly or lame. And that's perfectly alright. List your core fears on the paper. And be honest because that's the only way you can succeed.

The project I am working on is _____.

The list of what-if scenarios and core fears are:

What-if Scenarios/Failures	Core Fears
-	-
-	-
-	-

Congratulations on making this list! I hope you were honest and authentic about all the reasons that stop you from becoming the best version of yourself.

How Did You Become so Afraid?

Let's put the blame on your **subconscious mind** for all the fears. Shall we? This area of the brain stores all your fears.

Your subconscious mind stores all your memories and experiences. Whether you consciously remember them or not, these memories affect your body and control your thoughts and other impulses. The subconscious mind records memories from the moment of your birth and may also include memories of other lifetimes. **This data in the subconscious mind acts as a template or a blueprint instruction for determining your choices**. Until you learn to communicate with your subconscious mind, you will not be able to change the default template/blueprint of your life.

Say your default way of thinking includes statements like:
- I can't live alone.
- I excel in math.
- Darkness scares me.

These phrases/statements/opinions are your beliefs. And these beliefs form your default way of thinking.

Beliefs are solid ideas stored in the subconscious mind.

Beliefs (aka, your default way of thinking) are formed in childhood through your interactions with adults around you.

When you were growing up, if your parents kept telling you that you needed to embrace failure daily, then, as an adult, you show up in the world not being afraid to fail. You might fail in your ventures, and yet you spring right back up because your subconscious beliefs tell you that:

- Failure is normal and acceptable.
- Failure should be embraced every single day.
- Failure is never permanent.
- Failure constantly nudges you toward your destiny.

On the other hand, if your parents told you that failure should be avoided at all cost, your subconscious beliefs might sound like:

- Failure should be avoided.
- Only take on a new business if you can succeed.
- Either you are on top or at the bottom.
- Your value equals the money in your bank account.
- Once you fail, it takes years to build up again.

A collection of negative beliefs stored in the subconscious mind gives rise to core fears.

In creating the list of what-if scenarios and core fears, you have successfully uncovered the contents of your subconscious beliefs. These limiting beliefs prevent you from taking the next steps in your projects and your goals.

Continuing with the last example I shared with you, once I listed the what-if scenarios and the core fears, I then wrote the underlying beliefs.

My list looked something like this:

Core Fears	Subconscious Beliefs
- Fear of being judged	- My success is validated by something/someone outside of me. - I don't have anything of value to share.
- Fear of being a failure	- Failure should be avoided at all cost. - Failure equates to pain, and pain should be avoided at all cost.

Being aware of these beliefs is the first step in loosening the tight grip of fear of failure, and failure itself. You might have already heard that the subconscious mind doesn't question or reason with your beliefs. It is like a child, willing to believe whatever you may tell it.

Your turn to identify your limiting beliefs:

Core Fears	Subconscious Beliefs
-	-

-	-

Congratulations on completing the exercise and uncovering the hidden contents of your subconscious mind and the fear contents of your Mental Body.

Chapter 3 —

Common Blocks in an

"Overly Analytical"

Mental Body

In the last chapter, we looked at the "fear-based" contents of your mind. In this chapter, we will explore some of the most common blocks found in the overly analytical Mental Body.

You can think of these blocks as "limiting" mental attitudes that most overly analytical women are susceptible to. These inherent blocks/impediments include attitudes like perfectionism, controlling people, withholding communication, leaving conversations incomplete, not speaking your mind, fear of appearing vulnerable, feeling inferior, shame, guilt, etc.

One needn't be an overthinker to embody these limiting beliefs. However, these mental attitudes are most conspicuous in overanalyzers and overthinkers. You don't come into this world with limiting blocks/attitudes. However, by adopting and perpetuating an overanalyzing mindset, you tend to internalize these limiting behaviors without questioning them.

If you think of your Mental Body as a software program loaded into your brain, then, still following the analogy, these blocks and negative attitudes represent software bugs and glitches. A healthy and balanced Mental Body will run like a bug-free computer program.

When the mind is running on overdrive (as with overthinkers and overanalyzers), you can assume that there are bugs in the Mental Body's software, and they need to be fixed.

There are numerous bugs in the Mental Body software of the people who overanalyze. We will discuss the top six inherent bugs here:
1. Feelings of Inferiority (not-enough-itis).
2. Perfectionism.
3. Know-it-all Mindset.
4. Not Saying It Like It Is.
5. Lack of Authentic Communication.
6. The Need to Control.

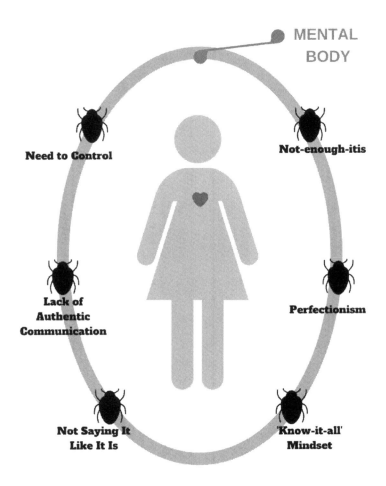

Mental Body Bug #1

"Not-enough-itis" and Its Antidote (Creative-itis)

I'm sure many folks can identify with feelings of being inferior, of "not being enough." Have you ever said the following to yourself? I am not:

- Beautiful enough.
- Thin enough.
- Rich enough.
- Capable enough.
- Smart enough.
- Successful enough.
- Enough of a mother/wife/daughter.
- Enough...

... Sure, you have, and the list probably goes on.

I have struggled with thoughts of inferiority for the longest time. I often felt that no matter what I did in the world, it would never be enough. I also know that the majority of my girlfriends struggle with thoughts of "not being enough," no matter how successful and brilliant they are. Thoughts of inferiority are like a disease in the Mental Body, and you must make a conscious effort to eradicate this affliction.

Not-enough-itis is also a cover-up for perfectionism, and it manifests in living up to a distorted standard—someone else's standard—of accomplishment and success. Instead of appreciating your uniqueness and strengths, you look to the outer world for validation, recognition, and acceptance. Unfortunately, no one in the world can validate your existence. You must do it on your own; you owe it to yourself.

When you compare yourself with others or hold yourself to the beauty standards established by social media, it is rather easy to fall into the trap of feeling like you're simply not enough. Can anyone feel sufficient by comparing themselves to Victoria Secret models? I know that I wouldn't.

Your sense of "being enough" can rarely come from anything outside of you. The responsibility to accept yourself lies squarely on your own two shoulders.

No fairy godmother is coming to tell you how beautiful, competent, intelligent, and capable you are. You need to accept these qualities in yourself.

Unless you accept yourself for who you are at your deepest level, you will always be looking for validation in the outside world and remain stuck in endless cycles of not being enough.

But how do you heal yourself from not-enough-itis, a disease highly prevalent in our culture?

The Antidote to Not-enough-itis

A few years back, in utter frustration and desperation, I said to myself, "There's got to be a way to get out this freaking not-enough-itis."
Through many trials and plenty of errors, I found a simple way to break out of this crazy bondage loop. But how?

Number one: be creative. I know this antidote may sound unbelievably simple, but I promise you that it's highly effective. When my ego begins playing the old recorded memories and thoughts of not-enough-itis, I don't argue with it. Instead, in such situations, I seek solace in creativity.

Now, creativity is a subjective term. It means different things to different people. What might be "oh-so creative" to me may fall flat for you. Explore what creativity means to you. Now, creative solutions can change from one scenario to another. In one situation, a brilliant idea might entail reaching out to 10 new clients, while in another scenario, it might mean spending quality time with a loved one, or making beautiful art; whatever it is, trust it and use it.

As an example, when thoughts of inferiority start swirling in my head, there are a few things I do.
- First, I recognize the trigger (that it's not-enough-itis).
- Second, I ask myself what creative solution I can call upon to address these thoughts. Sometimes, it's making a simple list of everything I have accomplished so far. Other times, I work on my

business plans. It depends on the issue at hand and what needs to be addressed.

- Third, I journal my feelings about the situation at hand, and then, surprisingly enough, my mind never fails to come up with creative solutions to help me move forward.

No one can tell you what a "perfect" creative solution looks like. You have to feel the resonance in your heart and act on the guidance you receive from your inner self.

Number two: practice self-acceptance. You need to remind yourself that it doesn't matter what the world thinks of you, what matters most is what you think of yourself. With all the love in your heart, give some to yourself. Give yourself a big hug. Why wouldn't you? There is no one—I mean, no one!—in this world of 7.5 billion people that resembles the magnificence of who you are. So, acknowledge yourself and accept yourself, right here and right now.

I often joke with my friends that if I had to marry a word, it would probably be "***acknowledgment***." When you acknowledge yourself for where you are, at the present moment in time, you open yourself to the richness of this word. I just had to point that out to you.

One of my favorite authors, Kris Carr, says, "Accepting yourself isn't about giving up or settling or throwing in the towel. No. Accepting yourself is about having your own back and never abandoning yourself."

Ask yourself:

- What am I not accepting about myself?
- Where am I disconnected from myself?
- Where am I not being my authentic self?
- What stops me from living an authentic life?
- Why am I afraid to be myself?

Your sense of disconnection comes from living an empty and meaningless life. If who you are on the inside doesn't match with how you appear and act, then that is a sign of inability to accept yourself. This is very important in becoming the best you can be.

Number three: cultivate courage. The word courage means "To speak one's mind by telling all that is in one's heart." In other words, speaking from your heart is what ordinary courage sounds like. Courage rarely feels comfortable because there is no guarantee how people will respond when you speak your truth.

While, superficially, courage feels "brave" and "gusty," on the inside, it creates the feeling of being authentic, of being aligned to who you truly are.

Next time you feel like you're just not enough, try out one of the three antidotes, or perhaps try all of them. See if that makes any difference.

Mental Body Bug #2

Perfectionism and its Antidote (Service to Others)

The majority of overthinkers and overanalyzers show signs of perfectionism to various degrees. Brene Brown calls perfectionism a "20-ton shield that you lug around, thinking that it will protect you when, in fact, it's the thing that's really preventing you from being seen and taking flight."

You know you have a perfectionist streak if you:

- Want everything perfect (like a perfect career/home/marriage).
- Have a loud inner critic.
- Struggle with making mistakes.
- Think and act in extremes (also called black/white thinking).
- Have difficulty finishing projects.
- Have trouble delegating.
- Set unrealistic standards for yourself and others.
- Are depressed by your unmet goals.
- Are not satisfied with anything less than perfect.

If you relate to any of these patterns, then I want to tell you—you are not alone in this struggle.

Brene Brown describes it best in her book "The Gifts of Imperfection." She says that perfectionism is the ultimate fear. "People who are walking around as perfectionists... They are ultimately afraid that the world is going to see them for who they really are, and they won't measure up."

She further adds that "Perfectionism is not about striving for excellence or healthy striving. It's a way of thinking and feeling that says this: If I look perfect, work perfect, and live perfect, I can avoid or minimize shame, blame, and judgment."

"Healthy striving is self-focused: 'How can I improve?'
Perfectionism is other-focused: 'What will they think?'"

There is something to be said about perfectionism. I feel it is beautiful that a part of us wants to excel and work toward becoming the best version of ourselves. That is noble.

However, when the drive to get everything perfect supersedes the desire to serve a greater cause, that's when perfectionism becomes an impediment in the journey to wholeness.

The Antidote to Perfectionism

So, how does one get over the perfectionism streak? Here are some of the suggestions that have worked for me:

Number one: make peace with your inner critic. Joke with it, laugh at it, poke fun at it. Take it seriously. Be vulnerable to it. Write a letter to it. Try ALL these things. Have a relationship with your inner critic; it might have so much personality that she deserves a name or a voice that belongs only to her. *Listen behind the sharp words of your inner critic for the love of doing things right.*

Number two: remind yourself that you are committing to live a real life, not a perfect life. A real life is messy, chaotic, and beautiful, and it makes you experience love, heartache, joy, disappointment, sadness, and all range of emotions. Your emotions are an integral part of your human experience. In fact, emotions make humans human.

As a perfectionist, you might run away from challenging emotions because they don't appear perfect. Please don't do that. Labeling moments as perfect or imperfect keeps you stuck in vicious loops of perfectionism. Learn to see and appreciate the beauty in chaos.

Number three: one of the most potent ways to overcome the perfectionist streak is to serve others. Add value in other people's lives. Focus on service, on truly being helpful. Allow yourself to disappear in the work, but make sure that your work aligns with your inner core. This is the doorway to greater effectiveness, and that magical state you call "flow." Be of service to *others*, instead of service to yourself.

When you serve others, the focus and the spotlight is no longer on you. The attention is on the work, and it is on other people. The inner critic doesn't feel incessantly loud because your focus is on creating value for other people, rather than being perfect. And even when you make mistakes, you will find it easier to let go and forgive yourself (a huge challenge for a perfectionist mind).

Sounds too good to be true? You bet it is.

In my own experience, the more I tapped into the feelings of serving others, the more I could let go of my perfectionist tendencies. My mind no longer shut down in brand-new circumstances. I could act in the face of unknown situations and still maintain inner balance. The mindset of serving others always puts me in my heart center, and when my operating system shifts from head to heart, I feel divinely guided in my work and interactions.

Hence, I fondly regard the *"service-to-others mindset"* as a *"Mental Body bypass tool."*

Dare yourself to be imperfect, even if it is for a few moments each day! You will find that even though you are imperfect, the sun will still rise the next morning, the flowers will still bloom, and the world will still carry on… just like it always has. So, relax! Allow yourself to just be! You don't have to carry the weight of this world on your shoulders, my dear friend. Let go of that armor of perfectionism.

Mental Body Bug #3

Know-it-all Mindset and its Antidote (Practicing Intellectual Humility)

Generally speaking, many women who overanalyze also have an insatiable appetite for knowledge and learning. Many of them are highly educated. They often pursue higher education, and might even get a Ph.D. Being a highly knowledgeable person is a big source of pride for most overly analytical thinkers.

I am not saying that all overthinkers have a know-it-all attitude. However, most overanalyzers have a proclivity towards a know-it-all mindset.

You know you have a know-it-all mindset when you:
- Don't listen to other people's ideas and suggestions.
- Think that your ideas are intellectually superior to everyone.
- Think that your approach is the *only* approach to get desired results.
- Are not open to feedback from other people.
- Are stuck in a problem and don't ask for help (usually because your overthinking mind has already convinced you that you will figure things out on your own).

The feeling of superior thinking is another manifestation of a know-it-all attitude.

Fortunately, you can change this mindset once you become aware of it. I remember a time when I had just started my meditation practice. I voraciously read books on meditation and spent as much time meditating as I possibly could. Few years in, I got cocky and thought that, perhaps, I knew everything there was to know about meditation. Talk about being arrogant and pretentious!

I forgot that no matter how much I read or meditated, my meditation practice will always keep evolving. Growth is never static. I didn't realize that meditation practice is a journey, not a destination. This was indeed a humbling realization for me.

Through many painful lessons, I was able to overcome the know-it-all mindset by:
- Letting go of the need to always be right.
- Having a willingness to hear (and embrace) other people's perspectives.
- Asking for help, feedback, and advice.
- Being curious in my interactions with people.
- Not making preconceived judgments or assumptions about people and situations in general.

There are still moments and days when I slip into the know-it-all mindset, but, thankfully, with enough practice, I can pull myself out of it with relative ease.

The Antidote to the Know-it-all Mindset*

Number one: practice humility. It starts with embracing behaviors and attitudes such as:

- Recognizing virtues and talents that others possess as they are, without being envious of those talents, particularly if recognizing other people have skill-sets that may currently surpass your own skill level.

- Recognizing the limits of your talents, ability, or authority and avoiding to reach for what is beyond practical reality in terms of fantasies, embellishments, or magical thinking. For example, would you refer to yourself as an Olympic gold-winning swimmer when you're just a casual swimmer at the community pool? Of course, you wouldn't.

- Knowing yourself and being authentic and true to yourself, all the while ignoring the need to compete with others but recognizing those skills or proficiencies in people around you that may inspire you or help you to become an improved person.

An honest and humble person would state the accurate facts of conditions in the moment as a true representation.

Number two: let go of the need to always be right. The "my way or the highway" thinking rarely works in reality. You can offer your insights, perceptions, and ideas to other people, but you can never force anyone to accept your ideologies. When you fundamentally accept that each person has free will and is free to choose their belief system, then you learn to respect their choices. You finally stop taking things personally and accept others for who they are and who they are not, thus learning to be humble.

When you have spent your entire life overanalyzing and being overly analytical, it can feel challenging to learn humility, to accept that others know more than you and that they could be better than you. Don't beat yourself up if you falter in practicing humility. The key is to recognize when you fall, and then to quickly rise back again.

*Source: www.energeticsynthesis.com

Mental Body Bug #4

"Not Saying It Like It Is" and Its Antidote (Staying True and Saying It Like It Is)

Another common bug in the Mental Bodies of women who overanalyze is the refusal to call things as they really are. Meaning, they don't speak up their mind. Often, women cover up their inner-most feelings and intentions in their interactions with other people around them.

Fear can stop you from speaking your truth. You might be afraid because:

- You think that your truth might offend people in your life.
- You think people won't love you if they knew your authentic core.
- You think that people in your life might leave you if they knew your real intentions.

Your analytical mind could even trick you into believing that people in your life can't handle your truth. You couldn't be more wrong about this.

Speak your truth, first with yourself, and then others, even if your voice shakes.

When you speak your truth, you release yourself from the bondage of suffering. And when you show up as your most authentic self, you unconsciously give other people permission to also show up as their authentic self. Authenticity is truly contagious. People are usually much more capable at handling truth than you give them credit for.

The Antidote to Not Saying It Like It Is

The one and only antidote to not saying it like it is would be to say it like it really is, truly is, to speak your mind.

Say what you mean, and mean what you say.

When you authentically communicate with other people, it creates a possibility of meaningful and honest relationships. When you speak your truth, it encourages other people to speak their truth.

Speak your mind, no matter how uncomfortable it makes you feel. As an example, if you're tongue-tied in business gatherings, then announce it to everyone prior to the meeting. "Hey, I tend to feel nervous during these group discussions, so I will share my thoughts at the end of our meeting or maybe through my notes." Sounds strange, I know, but this will help you to face your fears and avoid overthinking about your fears.

If you feel nervous on your first date, tell your date how you feel! Your date might be just as nervous, and this could be a fun ice-breaker!

Truth and humor go a long way in helping you to let go of your need to control situations.

When I started writing this book, the fear of imperfection had reared its ugly head more times than I like to admit. This fear made me stop in my tracks, and I often wondered about ways to get every detail perfect.

Then I reminded myself—say it like it is. And so, I made a few tweaks to the cover page of the book. I added a header (right above the title), calling this book part of "The Imperfectly Perfect Series." By addressing my fear of imperfection at the onset, I surrender my obsession with getting everything perfect.

By saying it like it is, I am willingly accepting a less-than-perfect outcome. I am embracing an imperfect outcome so that fear doesn't stop me from taking massive actions.

The idea is to find ways to say things as they are, as you see them, without lying or deception so that you are never stopped from taking necessary actions.

Mental Body Bug #5

The Lack of Authentic Communication and Its Antidote (Shine Your Authenticity)

Are you honest and transparent in all your conversations with your friends, family, colleagues, parents, or spouse? Can you answer this question with an undisputed "Yes?"

If not, then perhaps, you are transparent on a selective basis. That is, you communicate with transparency and honesty with some people, but with others, you hide your true self behind a smoke screen. Women who overthink lean toward being selectively transparent.

I have often wondered how overanalyzers can synthesize brilliant analysis, and yet falter when initiating authentic conversations.

In observing myself and others, I have discovered a few reasons that prevent overanalyzers from being authentic in their communication:

- Fears! Mainly, fear of speaking one's truth. Fear of potential heartache, pain, or discomfort. Fear of vulnerability. Fear of hurting other people. Fear of disagreement or arguments.
- Moving from head to heart is an enormous challenge for most overanalyzers; they feel safer in their intellect rather than dealing with raw emotions in relationships.
- They may not know how to initiate authentic conversations.

- Panic. They may not know how to just *be* with themselves or others.
- They don't realize the importance of authenticity in relationships. Perhaps they might not realize that authenticity is the foundation on which good relations are built.

Before I learned the importance of authenticity in communication and relations, the majority of my relationships sucked. They felt empty and meaningless, and I couldn't understand why. During this time, most of my conversations with other people also felt draining, which, in retrospect, makes perfect sense. When you have inauthentic conversations, you can't expect to feel fresh as a daisy. Right?

I wished that people had a sixth sense that enabled them to read my thoughts so I wouldn't have to open my mouth and excuse myself from potentially draining conversations. I used to fantasize that people should know my thoughts without me having to open my mouth.

Can you imagine how much confusion and discord such thinking created? No wonder my relationships sucked at that time!

Thankfully, I have learned the hard lesson of speaking my truth, no matter how uncomfortable it makes me feel.

The Antidote to the "Lack of Authentic Communication"

Number one: be honest and truthful with yourself. You can't embody authenticity unless you embrace it in yourself. This means that:

- You always speak your mind and tell the truth. Not because you *have to*, but because it's who you are.
- You walk away from people, situations, or groups that no longer resonate with you. This is not a judgment, but, rather, your inner discernment of being true to yourself.
- You no longer put a facade up for anyone. You are honest both on the inside and the outside.
- You tell the truths from your past, truths you might have been hiding, to other people.

Number two: commit to a heart-based communication. When you are speaking from a place of love and commitment, you are naturally authentic. This also means that when emotions like anger or frustration are running high, then you need to take a moment to step back, relax, and find your heart center before engaging in any conversations.

Number three: let your inner light shine. Meaning, don't withhold or edit the thoughts in your head. Say what you need to say in your relationships.

This may feel excruciatingly uncomfortable because a part of you may feel exposed. Your brain can trick you into believing that if you truly allow others to see you deeply, then you won't be loved or accepted. This is a common pitfall, and I fell for it many times. Eventually, I realized that people who genuinely love me would keep loving me, perhaps even more than before for my authenticity. The superficial friendships will die their own death anyway, so no need to burden myself with lies and discomfort.

Rather than talking in your head, talk to people in your life. Let them know your dreams, your aspirations, what brings you joy, and what doesn't. Connect with people, especially those closest to you. I assure you, you will experience joy and freedom that you never knew was possible in relationships.

Your authenticity will open doors for you that you didn't even know existed. Really embrace that. In this day and age, I feel it's refreshing to be authentic.

Mental Body Bug #6

The Need to Control and Its Antidote (Surrender)

Please forgive me for saying this, but I am convinced that women who overthink and overanalyze are the quintessential control freaks. They yearn to control people and places and events and situations in their lives. In fact, it is the desire to control everything that drives women to overthink and overanalyze.

Sometimes, your controlling behavior may be unconscious and hidden behind layers of worry, panic, and anxiety. Generally, you may find it easy to observe the thought patterns that stem from these emotions in your life. However, **controlling thoughts and controlling behaviors are rarely self-evident.** You may tell yourself that you never control anyone or anything, but if you start to dig deep and observe your behaviors and thoughts, the controlling aspects will become conspicuous.

Wouldn't it be flattering if everything in the world revolved around you? That you were the focal point of this universe? Well, my dear friend, I hate to burst your bubble—you're not.

You can't control every person, event, or situation, no matter how much you want to. You can offer your ideas to another person, but you can't impose your thinking on them; not always. People might be open and willing to hear your ideas and beliefs, or they might shut you down.

You need to respect, accept, and honor how other people choose to live their lives and how they react to your advice and suggestions. Even if you know better, you need to mind your own business and not impose your will on others, be it your children or colleagues or anyone else you hold dear. ***When you respect this fundamental truth, you stop wanting to control people in your life.***

However, what you can control is—yourself. You can control how you respond to any situation or event in your life. You have the power to choose, and no one can take it away.

I was a control freak, and I didn't even see it until I started a regular meditation practice and became aware of my thought patterns. My compulsive need to control would usually manifest as:

- Panic, especially when situations didn't work out as expected.
- Anger, when others didn't comply with my ideas and beliefs.
- Resentment, when I saw that others achieved more.
- Fear, when I couldn't find a way out of my predicaments.

I probably had an obsessive-compulsive disorder to control everything in my life! It was mentally exhausting. I observed that my need to control stopped me from exploring new opportunities and experiences because my intellectual analysis could never predict the outcome of new realities. Hence, this limiting mindset kept me safe in my little world.

To step into the unknown, you have to give up your need to control. In other words, you can either explore the unknown or you can quench your thirst for control. They cannot co-exist.

If you want to practice giving up control, here are a few suggestions. You can start implementing them in your life today:

- Allow people to be who they are and who they are not, without judging them.
- Accept yourself as you are—not when you are 10 pounds lighter/heavier or when you have completed your overdue Ph.D. thesis or cleaned all the laundry.
- Embrace your weaknesses like you embrace your strengths.
- Be flexible to the possibilities that always exist around you. When you become attached to an outcome, you can't stay flexible. *I always remind myself to have preferences and not attachments.*

The Antidote to the "Need to Control"

Number one: learning to surrender. For the longest time, I thought of surrender as admitting defeat and giving up. I thought of surrender as a weakness. Given my overly analytical mind, it took me forever to experience what it meant to surrender.

Let's discuss what surrender is NOT! It's not:

- Giving up.
- Stopping the pursuit of your dreams.

- Doing nothing to solve your problems.
- A passive state of being.

What surrender does mean is that:
- You give your very best to all situations and commitments, and then leave things to a higher power.
- You learn to accept that when things don't work out the way you wanted them to be, it's because God has a better plan for you.

If you are fighting any situation in your life, then you are probably not surrendering.

Surrender means giving your hundred percent to your work, life, and relationships, and then leaving it all to a higher power, trusting that the circumstances will unfold in the highest good for all.

Number two: remind yourself that a higher power is always working through your life. The power that makes the world go around, keeps Earth in its orbit, and makes the sun shine every day can also work wonders in your life—but only if you allow it to. You need to trust this power.

That's why the seemingly happy-go-lucky people appear to sail through life without too many hiccups. They have intrinsically honed the art of surrender, regardless of whether they realize it or not.

Chapter 4 — Tools for the Mental Body Reset

In the last two chapters, you have uncovered your core fears and beliefs that keep you stuck in a familiar, uncomfortable rut. You also learned about the common blocks in the overly analytical Mental Body.

By default, the Mental Body in most analytical women is overstimulated. This overstimulation can manifest as:

- Obsessive-compulsive thinking.

- Looping thoughts (thinking about one thing over and over again).

- Scattered thoughts (thinking about many things at once).

Common blocks in overly analytical Mental Bodies that we discussed in the last chapter *perpetuate* the overstimulation of the Mental Body.

One of the most effective ways to reset the Mental Body is to actively reprogram the contents of your subconscious mind (the brain's hard drive).

The main function of the subconscious mind is data storage. Recognize that your **subconscious mind is also a non-reasoning mind,** which means that it lacks the ability to comprehend the stored data. You have to program your brain's hard drive such that the stored data aligns with your goals and dreams.

In this chapter, we will discuss the following tools that you can use to reprogram the contents of your subconscious mind and reset the Mental Body:

1. Affirmations.
2. Daily Meditation.
3. Meditation for Removing Core Fears.
4. Journaling.
5. Celebrating and Tracking Daily Failures.
6. Phone Detox.

Tool #1: Affirmations

The subconscious mind functions according to the law of attraction. It examines, classifies, and stores information like a computer hard drive. The subconscious mind doesn't discriminate the stored data. Additionally, it doesn't know the difference between when you're thinking and when you're dreaming; it perceives both realities as identical.

The information stored on your brain's hard drive creates your reality. If you want to experience a new reality, you must download new data (information) into the hard drive. Your subconscious mind stores data in the form of images. To experience a new reality, your subconscious mind must have images that correspond with this new reality.

Affirmations can be the single most effective tool for changing your subconscious beliefs, stances, and limiting thought patterns.

A few years back, while working on a photography project, I felt blocked in my creativity, and I didn't know how to unblock it. I thought that, perhaps, either one is born creative, or one isn't. And I just belonged to the latter group.

This was before I learned about how the subconscious mind works. Once I realized the power of affirmations, I started affirming to myself that "I am a creative genius."

Every day, at least three to four times, I would repeat to myself that I was a creative genius. After several months of repetition, I was shocked that I started acting as a creative person. As an example, I enrolled for piano lessons. I signed-up for sketching and woodworking workshops! For someone who thought they weren't born with the creativity gene, this was indeed a pleasant surprise.

As I developed my artistic skills, my friends and family members started complimenting me on how creative I was! I was able to change my long-held subconscious belief through the repetitive use of an affirmation. If this change can happen to me, then it surely can happen to you.

Affirmations (also called positive declarations) can alter your subconscious beliefs and your limiting thought patterns.

In Chapter 2, you worked through an exercise of identifying your limiting beliefs (that is, your default way of thinking). I shared the following list of my core fears:

Core Fears	Limiting Beliefs (Default Way of Thinking)
- Fear of being judged	- My success is validated by something outside of me. - I don't have anything of value to share.
- Fear of being a failure	- Failure should be avoided at all cost.

	- Failure equates to pain, and pain should be avoided at all cost.

Once you have identified a limiting belief, the next step is to write down affirming statements that negate and neutralize your default way of thinking.

For example, one of my limiting beliefs was that failure should be avoided at all cost.

To counter this belief, I made a list of positive affirmations:
- I am comfortable with making mistakes.
- I make mistakes every day.
- Failure leads me to my destined goal.

There is no right or wrong way of choosing an affirmation. Choose words and sentences that resonate with you and evoke a strong, positive response in your heart.

Once I completed my list, this is what I got:

Limiting Beliefs (Default Way of Thinking)	New Affirmations
- My success is validated by something outside of me.	- I am a success. - I allow myself to be successful.

- Failure should be avoided at all cost.	- I am always comfortable with making mistakes. - I am growing past my mistakes. - I make new mistakes every day.

Now you may write one or more affirmations to counter your own negative beliefs. Play around and see what rings true in your heart. Take charge!

Write down powerful affirmations for each negative belief you wrote in Chapter 2.

Limiting Beliefs	New Affirmations
-	-
-	-
-	-

Once you have written down the affirmations, the most important work starts now.

- Read out each sentence for at least three to five times every day for approximately 30 days, preferably longer if you can.
- Be **present** with the words as they come out of your mouth. Being present means that you can't be thinking of your dinner plans or your business trip or the weekend plans. Your complete attention and focus need to be on the words you are saying.

- **Visualize** your goals. Visualize the dreams that you wish to experience. Visualization is a powerful tool to program the subconscious mind because when you visualize, you send (and download) images to your subconscious mind.

You will know you are done with an "affirmation list" when you no longer think in your old ways.

Affirmations have now become an integral part of my Mental Body healing and reset. My list includes 10-15 affirmative declarations that I say out loud every single day. I find it interesting that there is always a noticeable difference in the energies of the days when I say my affirmations and when I don't.

On the days I do my affirmations and I am present to hear the words, I have noticed that:

- I start to think in terms of my affirmations. I know this might sound spooky, but that is—I promise you—not the case. For example, I would be reading something, and, all of a sudden, an affirmation from my list would pop into my head, like: "I am a success. I allow myself to be successful."
- There is an underlying harmony to my days. I know it's hard to put something intangible to words, and this is the best way I can put it.
- Affirmations slow down my mind and help me to stop obsessively thinking.
- Affirmations protect my mind from gloomy and depressing thoughts. In fact, they keep my mind uplifted because I know my

mind is continually attracting all the things that I want to experience in my life

List of Affirmations

Some of you might be working with affirmations for the first time, so I wanted to share a few examples. Here are some powerful affirmations that you can choose from while creating your affirmations list:

Financial Success

- I am the Source of my Abundance.
- I am Abundantly provided for when I follow my Heart and the Highest Purpose.
- I am always in the Right Place at the Right Time, and everything works out more than fine.
- I am a Success! I allow myself to Feel and Experience my Success.
- I am Unique, and I Honor my Special Skills and abilities in Service to Others.

Love/Relationship Success

- I am in a Relationship that brings me Joy and Comfort in every way.
- I am willing to see how Beautiful and Attractive I am to Others.
- I am willing to allow Others to Love me and be Close to Me.
- I am Loved for my Authenticity. I express my Authenticity to Others, and especially my Partner.
- I am deeply Nourished in all my Relationships.

Emotional Wellbeing

- I am the Power, Master, and Cause of my Emotions.

- I am the Power, Master, and Cause of my Mind.

- I am Integrated, Whole, and Balanced.

- I am Innocent. I Forgive myself Utterly and Completely.

- I am Congruent, Consistent, Centered, and Responsible for all aspects of my life.

- I am filled with Appreciation and Gratitude for all the things in my life.

I am hoping that these examples give you clarity on how to structure your own affirmations.

Tool #2: Daily Meditation

One of the cornerstones of an analytical mind is super-fast mental processing. Analytical women are blessed with a quick brain that processes data in milliseconds. While others might be still figuring out the details, these intellectual geniuses may have already thought through 13 different solutions in their head.

Meditation is anything but fast mental processing.

If you open any book on meditation, you will find that the primary aim of meditation is to still the mind into deep silence. In a way, it might seem like meditation is the antithesis to the very nature of an analytical mind, and yet it is one of the most effective and profound tools for healing an overactive mind.

While sitting in silence and doing nothing can feel like a punishment, it is also what saves you from the dissecting nature of your intellectual mind. Meditation allows pure feelings to register in the body and helps the overly busy mind to cease the endless chatter.

Choose a Meditation That Works for You

There are endless resources on meditation available online these days. It really doesn't matter what form of meditation you choose because all will work fine.

You can explore meditation forms such as Kundalini meditation, the Wim Hof Method, walking meditation, guided meditation, chanting, sitting in silence, listening to sounds of nature, or gazing into a candle flame.

If sitting in silence doesn't resonate with you, try putting on some light background music and see if that makes any difference. You may explore painting, sketching, or even gardening as a form of meditation. Playing a musical instrument can also be a meditative experience.

Just as no two people are alike, no two meditation styles are similar. While one meditation technique might work brilliantly for one person, it may do nothing for another. Choose a meditation that matches your frequency.

The goal of meditation is to still the mind into silence. The path you choose to get to that stillness is unique to you.

Some of my favorite ways to silence my mind include gently gazing into the heart of a candle, listening to the sound of rain or flowing water, and counting breaths: breathe in and hold to a count of eight seconds, then start releasing your breath to a count of eight, and repeat.

The reason meditation works wonders for the Mental Body is that:

- *Meditation slows down the overactive mind.* The constant activity or busyness of an analytical brain keeps the brainwaves in a Beta state. You reach this brain state when you are alert, engaged in something like problem solving, judging a situation, or making decisions. Ideally, you want to consciously shift the brainwaves from a Beta to an Alpha wave frequency, which is the brain's state when you are relaxed and contemplative. Slowing down the mental processes helps in a better use of your brain's computer. Your brain can access deeper levels of information from your subconscious mind in the Alpha state.

- *Meditation helps to reset the default emotional responses.* One of the most effective ways to reset your default emotional responses is through meditation (more about this in the next section).

Tool #3: Meditation for Removing Core Fears

Over the years, I have explored many different forms of meditations. One form that is highly effective in healing the core fears is the Core Fear Removal Invocation. This meditation works wonders in healing and releasing the fears stored in your subconscious mind.

In 2017, I made a commitment to set up a daily practice of the Core Fear Removal meditation for 30 days. The invocation took less than three minutes, yet I was shocked to experience how effective and powerful it was.

To practice this meditation, read the following prayer aloud, preferably before going to bed and upon waking up.

Beloveds, I call forth My God Self, The Master Christos Collective serving the Law of One, My personal evolution support teams and Ascension healing teams.

Please install the latticework of light into my mind grid field and emotional field to remove all fear-based programs and artificial programs.

I Request the Core Fear Matrix Removal Program.

I ask first for general clearing of all fear-based programs that are hindering my spiritual growth and Ascension.

You may feel them moving out the top of your head or body. If you feel specific fears that you know about yourself, request them to be removed and identify them specifically to the Christos Masters to remove. The more specific you can identify the fear programming, the better.

NOTE — You can write a list of your fears, whatever they may be. Below is an example version, but your list should match fears specific to you. This is what the list should look like.

Please remove the fear of:
-   Fear of failure (example).
-   Fear of success (example).
-   Fear of the unknown (example).
-   Fear of being seen in the world (example).
-   Fear of being alone (example).
-   Fear of death (example).
-   Fear of survival (example).
-   Fear of …
-   Fear of …

I request that my Teams focus on my Physical Body and ask them to remove any and all fear-based and Mind Control programs lodged there.

I Request that you clear and heal my Etheric Body and remove any fear-based programs that are blocking me.

I request that you clear and heal my Astral Body and remove all fear-based programs and spiritual weeds from my Astral, or Emotional Body.

I request that you clear and heal my Mental Body and remove all thought forms of an imbalanced and negative nature.

I request to clear and heal my Spiritual Body fully, totally, and completely.

I Ask that the fear programs be completely removed from my Soul and from my blueprint and the Akashic Records. I give full permission for my God self to do this now. I thank the Christos Masters and my healing team for this healing and support.

Thank you. Thank you. Thank you.

A few notes about this meditation:

- As you read through the invocation, notice how it addresses removing fear from all the four bodies: Physical, Mental, Emotional, and Spiritual.

- If you visualize the Mental Body as a matrix, then think of this meditation as pulling out the fear-based weeds, or bugs, if you will, from the matrix.
- After practicing the meditation for 30 days, check in with yourself if you need to update your list of fears. Perhaps you have noticed that you no longer feel the old fears with the intensity you used to, or probably you no longer feel them at all. Update your list if need be. Maybe there is a deeper layer of fears that are now surfacing for clearing? Pay attention to your inner thoughts and guidance here.

Core Fear Removal has been part of my daily meditation routine since 2017. In my experience, it is one of the most potent prayers for releasing fear programs. I use it consistently to keep a check on the fear programs.

As a side note, please check if this meditation resonates with your heart at this time. If so, I would suggest starting with a 30-day practice. If not, then feel free to skip or come back to it whenever you feel ready.

*Source: www.energeticsynthesis.com

Tool #4: Journaling

Journaling is an excellent tool for mental clarity and aligning your head and heart. It also happens to be my favorite.

Women who overanalyze and overthink tend to have a lot of thoughts, very often. As in—a lot! It gets to a point where it becomes overwhelming. The need to control things (even if only mentally) is often quite intense for these beauties. They will go through a hundred different scenarios in their head before zeroing down on that one "perfect" approach. It is relatively easy for them to get caught up in their thinking so much that they lose sight of the big picture.

When your brain is continuously moving from one thought to another at a fast speed, it is nearly impossible to get clarity in your thinking. And that's where journaling can work like a charm.

The simple act of journaling in cursive hand forces the brain waves to slow down considerably. While you might be able to think at a supersonic speed, you can only write so fast.

Slowing down your brain activity helps your mind connect with your breath and your heart. This gives much-needed mental rest to your overworked overthinking mind.

When you journal, you become fully aware of your thoughts and your thought analysis.

There have been countless times when I was overwhelmed, thinking that I had to sort through a million things to reach a decision. In times like those, when I sat down to journal, it took no more than half a page of writing to clear my head. Even now, when my mind gets overwhelmed and starts making a fuss about little things, I know it is time to journal. In the last few years, journaling has become my go-to tool in times of mental and emotional distress.

As you start to journal, you might notice that your thoughts are disjointed. You might jump from writing about groceries to professing your love for your nieces, from complaining about the cold weather to your work assignments, and then shift to writing about what makes you happy and what makes you sad—all that is quite alright.

My journal looks like an amalgamation of highly disjointed thoughts. Just this morning, I wrote about visiting South of France this year, starting a new work project, attending a birthday party, and finished with the emotional meltdown I had two days before. My thoughts were all over the place, and yet they weaved together to make a beautiful mess!

How I Got Started in Journaling and What It Did for Me

A few years back, I came across the book called "The Artist's Way" by Julia Cameron. The foundation of the book is a daily practice called "Morning Pages." Writing three pages of a longhand stream of consciousness first thing in the morning; that is what constitutes as Morning Pages.

According to Julia Cameron, "There is no right or wrong way to do Morning Pages. You basically write three pages of whatever comes to your mind. These pages are not for public consumption. And if your head tells you 'I don't know what to write,' then you write 'I don't know what to write.'"

When I picked up the book, I desperately needed a breakthrough in a photography project that I was working on at that time. My extremely analytical brain was skeptical; how could writing three pages help me overcome a creative hump? I was desperate and looking for a breakthrough, so, with nothing to lose, I went all in.

For the first few days, my brain couldn't come up with anything to write. And so, I wrote, "I have nothing to write" on three pages of my journal, over and over again, day after day. I persisted. By the end of the fourth day, my brain turned on and I had so much to write that even three pages didn't seem enough.

Over the next few weeks and months, I got to know my thoughts and my beliefs at a more intimate level and in black and white. The ritual of Morning Pages gave me an opportunity to learn about the contents of my brain: how the complex neural networks in my mind were connected, and why I thought the way I did.

Very quickly, three pages turned into seven pages, which quickly became 20 pages. Before I knew it, I was in love with the ritual of Morning Pages.

Then something happened.

I noticed that while writing in cursive hand, I could never write something that wasn't in sync with my heart.

In other words, I couldn't lie to myself in my journal.

Whenever I tried to write something that was not aligned with me, I would hear my heart scream out, "No, no, no! This is not true! Cancel that out!'

The Morning Pages honed my intuition.
And, best of all, this way of journaling helped me hear the messages from my heart, loud and clear.

To this day, whenever I feel overwhelmed due to my overthinking tendencies, I go back to my journal to find clarity. It gets me out of my head and into my heart, helping me to see things clearly.

Tool #5: Celebrating and Tracking Daily Failures

A few years back, while I was peeling through the many layers of fears, clearly seeing my failures, I came across an article on Sara Blakely, the self-made billionaire who founded Spanx.

In the article, Sara talked about her relationship with failures. Sara shared that when she was younger, her dad would encourage her and her brother to fail. Every week at the dinner table, Sara's dad would ask her what she had failed at. She said her dad would give her a high five if she had something spectacular to share and would be disappointed if she had nothing to share.

Sara shared that this helped her re-frame her relationship with failing. Instead of looking at failure as an outcome, she labeled failure as "avoidance of stepping into the unknown." Meaning: being afraid to launch into something that you are not comfortable with.

Instead of failure being the final outcome, it meant not trying new things and gaining new experiences.

I remember when I first read the article; I thought this was pure genius. And then I wished my parents had incorporated the same in my upbringing.

While I couldn't go into the past and change the way I had been raised, I did the next best thing possible: I became my own parent. I started asking myself every day: What did you fail at today?

In the beginning, there were days when I embraced failure with open arms. And then there were times when I didn't want to entertain any failure; I just ignored it. Little did I know, this simple step of embracing daily failures would make everything much better, fairly quickly.

I remember, a year or so after I started practicing this acceptance of daily failures, I began tracking all the different ways I failed in a mobile app called HabitShare.

The following screenshot is from September, 2018. The green circles indicate the days when I dared to fail at least once, the red circles for days when I missed the challenge, and the grey circles represent no entries.

TRACKING DAILY FAILURE

< My Habits   **My Habits**   Edit

What did you fail at today?
Streak: +3 | Overall: 34% | 1 Friend

< September 2018 >

SU	MO	TU	WE	TH	FR	SA
						1
2	3	4	5	6	7	8
9	10	11	12	13	14	15
16	17	18	19	20	21	22
23	24	25	26	27	28	29
30						

1. Didn't have many friends to tag in Linkedin

2. I tried many times

6. Super duper failure

My Habits   Friends   Messages   Settings

Some of my failure experiments were silly, like asking random strangers for a five-dollar bill, asking random strangers if they would want to pay for my coffee or lunch, and sometimes just making conversation with a cute guy. Because … why not?

One time I even dared myself to ask a stranger to let me taste the ramen soup he was having! I was convinced that he was going to give me a puzzled look and say, "Heck, no!" But he was kind enough to say "yes, to my big surprise. In other failure experiments, I dared myself to speak up my truth and embrace my imperfect self in all its glory.

These small, seemingly inconsequential daily failures gave me an experience of what it means to stand in uncertainty, even if it was is only for a few seconds. When you make a random request of a stranger, for a moment, you have no idea how they are going to react. The outcome of the request feels unpredictable and the uncertainty feels uncomfortable.

The practice of tracking daily failures showed me in black and white that growth happens when you step outside of your comfort zone.

Learning to embrace uncertainty and experiencing random acts of kindness from random strangers has been a blessing in disguise of these failed experiments. I always knew that growth could only happen outside of my comfort zone. And yet it wasn't until I intentionally embraced these uncomfortable moments on a daily basis that I really started to appreciate the wisdom and truth of these words.

It is one thing to *know* something, and quite another to fundamentally *register* it as a truth in your whole being. I felt that these daily failure experiments gave me an opportunity to see failure as part of the process, but at a much deeper level.

Tracking my daily failures allowed the analytical side of me to relax and let go a little bit. ***There was always a surprise element to my daily failures, one I would always be looking forward to.***

The habit of tracking daily failures was one of the best gifts I ever gave to myself.

Tool #6: Phone Detox

You might be thinking, "What does phone detox have to do with slowing down the mental processing?" Well, actually, quite a bit.

Most of us carry a smartphone with us 24/7. From the moment you wake up to the time you sleep, your smartphone is always in your sight, if not in your hands. Over the last decade, the reliance on phones has become second nature.

Through your smartphone, you are continually bombarded with information. Everything is vying for your attention, be it the constant social media feed, world news, Netflix shows, YouTube videos, celebrity gossip, or something else entirely. In fact, sometimes you might stream or read information that you don't even need or care for!

Unfortunately, this dump of information doesn't do any good for your brain. If anything, it keeps your brain stuck in the Beta brainwaves (an overstimulated Mental Body). This is precisely the brainwave frequency that keeps you stuck in your overthinking ways.

Limiting the use of your phone shields your brain from a constant shelling, from information and mentally stimulating frequencies. In today's day and age, staying away from phone also helps in keeping the mind focused on one thing at a time.

A regular practice of phone detox gives your mind much-needed rest to contemplate and wonder.

Here's how I incorporate phone detox in my day-to-day schedule: I turn off my phone once I reach home after work—unless, of course, I am expecting very important calls. I figured that since I am not a president of some country (just yet), there is nothing so critical that needs an immediate answer. Things can wait. The absence of a phone (or, to be more precise, absence of frivolous distractions) allows me to work on my projects uninterrupted. It gives me an opportunity to unwind and reflect on the day, allowing my mind to shift gears to a more relaxed state of being.

Section 3: Removing Fear From the Emotional Body

Chapter 5 — Getting to Know the Emotional Body

When I was growing up, I used to hear the term "emotional intelligence." It was thrown around a lot, and I always used to wonder what the heck it meant. The only memory I have of this term is from early childhood: when I was little, I would throw a lot of tantrums and my dad would often tell me that I needed to learn to be "emotionally intelligent." I always used to side-line his feedback.

Truth be told, I had no idea what it meant to be emotionally intelligent. Did it mean that I zip up my mouth and not speak up? Or did it mean to let people be themselves and find the middle ground?

It wasn't until 2014 that I connected the dots and figured that there must be something I needed to do about my emotional health.

Emotional healing starts with getting to know yourself and your emotions, and observing how you react in sticky and not-so-sticky situations.

I used to hate feeling my emotions, and I would run away from them all the time. I would overeat, oversleep, and overdo anything and everything to escape them. This continued until I realized that unless I made peace with my feelings, I was going to keep running in circles, achieving nothing.

I once read a book that suggested that an emotion is simply "energy in motion." It is you who choose to label your emotions as good and bad, positive and negative, icky and not-icky. If you can simply look at your emotions as messages from your body, you will be much more evolved in your emotional being.

Until that point, the only emotion that I had really known was anger. For an analytical person like myself, emotions just felt unnecessary. I knew which experiences (and emotions) brought me joy and which ones didn't. And I did my very best to stay away from unpleasant situations (and hence unpleasant emotions).

This was until I was brought down by those intense fears, especially the fear of failing, while learning stock trading.

If you feel overwhelmed by your emotions and run away from them, or, worse, don't acknowledge their existence, then it's a potential sign that your Emotional Body needs some attention.

If you are someone who has never allowed yourself to feel the full range of your emotions, then it can be terrifying to even think about acknowledging the sensations of your body. The best piece of advice I would offer is to never judge your emotions. It's human to feel sadness, rage, fear, anxiety, happiness, love, and the whole gamut of emotions.

Brene Brown says that you can't selectively numb emotions. You can't say—here's anger, here's sadness; I don't want to feel it. She says that when you numb sadness, you numb joy and happiness as well.

Your willingness to explore your emotions, regardless of how intense they feel, starts to open a pathway to healing. Like all things in life, the more you see something for what it is, the less charge it holds on you. When you validate your emotions and give yourself permission to feel all range of emotions without judgment, you start the process of developing emotional resilience.

Once you start to explore your emotional terrain, you get to uncover your deep-seated beliefs and thought patterns. Your emotions stem from your beliefs, and when your emotions create chaos, chances are that you are holding on to beliefs that are not serving you well.

As an example, say that one of your core beliefs is that "the world is not a safe place." You might respond with fear and panic at the thought of moving out of your hometown. Now, unless you change your core belief from "the world is not a safe place" to "the world is a safe place," then your emotional response to independently exploring new countries and exotic destinations is probably going to remain the same. That is, you will continue to respond with fear and panic.

The beauty of emotional work is that you not only get to uncover your innermost thoughts, emotions, and beliefs, but also develop an ability to change them. And, as you change the way you think, you change the way you feel—through your emotional responses.

Chapter 6 — Fear and Its Other Emotional Friends

Fear, whether it's rational or irrational, rarely exists in isolation.

When you start exploring your deep-seated fears, you will notice that they are often covered by layers of secondary emotions, such as anger or shame or regret, maybe guilt or hopelessness.

As an example, one of my dear friends, John, once shared with me that he often felt regret and sadness for not starting his own company. As we spoke about his situation, I nudged him to look deeper, beyond the immediate feelings of regret and sadness. As he reflected on his state of mind, he uncovered that the main reason he didn't start a company was that he was afraid to fail.

John had been beating up himself and feeling regret and remorse for not taking any action. He observed how the fear of failure had played out not only in starting his company, but also in many other aspects of his life, such as home, job, and personal relationships. When John saw how fear of failure had been running his life, he decided to embrace failure, rather than remain paralyzed by it. He was able to let go of regret and sadness, enabling himself to become an owner of a thriving business.

John's secondary emotions (of regret and sadness) were a cover-up for his deep-seated fear of being a failure. Once he saw the root cause of his issue, he was able to let go of the recurring thoughts of regret and sadness. This case study clearly shows the power of observing and acknowledging your emotions, as it allows you to unravel the hidden fears behind the plethora of your emotions.

Do you feel remorse, guilt, anger, or any other similar emotion on a *consistent basis*? If so, is there an underlying fear that you are refusing to look at?

The best way to gauge whether an emotion is a cover-up for fear or not is to pay attention to how frequently it shows up.

Fear is often accompanied by secondary emotions such as:
- Anger/rage.
- Guilt/shame.
- Sadness/unhappiness.
- Anxiety.
- Regret/resentment.

- Hopelessness, and the likes.

Do you feel any of the emotions listed above? Is there any emotion that comes up consistently in your life? When you feel the same emotion repeatedly, chances are that it is a cover-up for a deep-seated fear.

From the image below, is there one or more secondary emotion that you feel on a consistent basis?

Once you start identifying your emotions, then you can work your way back to how they might be a cover-up for your fears.

Chapter 7 — Tools for the Emotional Body Reset

At the heart of the Emotional Body Reset is giving yourself permission to feel all range of emotions without ANY judgment.

Can you feel anger, joy, sadness, rage, or resentment without any judgment? Or do you judge yourself when you feel angry or sad or jealous? Perhaps you tell yourself that you shouldn't be feeling any negative emotions? That, somehow, it's wrong to be sad or angry?

When you start acknowledging your emotions, you stop running away from them. And when you stop running away from them, you finally give yourself permission and space to change the way you respond to your emotional challenges. The idea is not to submit yourself to your emotions, but, rather, to see them, accept them, and hear their message (if they have any), so that you can do something about them.

As an example, let's say one of your friends makes you feel jealous. Instead of running away from the fact that you are jealous, stop and accept this emotion without judgment. Once you accept how you feel, the next logical question to ask is: what are you jealous about? Is it your friend's big flashy house or your friend's collection of Louis Vuitton bags? Perhaps your friend has all the things that you wouldn't give yourself permission to buy? So, your friend is perhaps only a mirror through which you see yourself? Once you identify the root cause of your emotion, you then have the power to change it.

However, you can't get to the root cause of your emotions unless you:

- Accept your emotions without any judgment.
- Give yourself permission to completely feel all your emotions.
- Are willing to look at the "why" behind your emotions.
- Are willing to look at your beliefs that trigger emotional storms.

I often felt that my own judgments of my negative emotions were the greatest impediment in my journey to emotional healing and wellness. I wish that I had learned early on to acknowledge all of my feelings and accept them without any judgment.

In this chapter, we will explore the following tools for the Emotional Body reset:

1. Exploring Emotions Through Journaling.
2. Resetting the Default Emotional Responses With Meditation.
3. Developing Emotional Resilience.
4. Building a Support Tribe.

5. Practicing Gentleness and Neutrality.

6. Learning to Nurture the Inner Self.

Tool #1: Exploring Emotions Through Journaling

If you're someone who has never allowed yourself to feel your emotions freely, then it can be terrifying to even think about acknowledging them. And that's where journaling can help you thread the waters of your inner psyche.

Overthinkers easily get overwhelmed by the intensity or range of their emotions. Rather than exploring their feelings, they might choose to ignore them altogether. I know I did that all the time.

When I first started journaling, I would write about mundane things, like how my day went, the kind of interactions I had with people, things I learned during the day, and so on.

Once I formed the habit of journaling and felt safe in my journal, I then started writing about the different emotions I experienced on a day-to-day basis. At first, I was surprised to notice that I could feel a wide range of emotions. Later, I was shocked to uncover how deeply I felt these emotions. On a scale of 1 to 10, the intensity of my feelings was probably 11.

The more I wrote in my journal about my emotions, the easier it became to navigate the challenging emotional situations I encountered on a day-to-day basis.

The process of writing gave me clarity on how I felt, how I thought, what I was okay with, and what I was not okay with. ***Writing helped me establish my personal boundaries***, first on paper, and then with people in the real world.

Think of a healthy personal boundary as a circle or a bubble around you that you've established to protect yourself from being manipulated, used, or violated by others. It is your boundary that lets people know which behaviors you will tolerate and which ones you won't. When you're clear about who and what you are, it is much easier to have direct, honest, and open communication with people in your life.

If you are committed to emotional clarity and healing, then pick up a pen and paper and start writing.

Even if all you can think is, "I have nothing to write," then that is exactly what you need to write. The point is not to stop in the face of inner resistance, but to push through it, and to stop analyzing. Don't worry about whether you are doing journaling the "right" way or the "wrong" way because your inner self will never lead you down the "wrong" path.

There is no right or wrong way to write in your journal. You only need to be willing to journal with honesty, staying true to yourself as you write down your thoughts and feelings.

I knew nothing about emotional clarity, let alone emotional healing, when I started journaling. It was an organic outcome of a consistent journaling practice.

The habit of daily journaling gave me a sense of emotional stability, a sense of clarity and emotional well-being that I had never experienced (in a particularly tangible way) throughout my life. For an excruciatingly analytical person, such as myself, journaling provided a space of calmness, tranquility, and peace for my Mental Body and Emotional Body. It made me feel as if all my life's challenges were figureoutable.

Like I mentioned before, journaling forces your brain to slow down considerably. While you may be able to think at a speed of 100 miles per hour, you might only be able to write a maximum of 20 words per minute!

When your brain is moving from one thought to another at a fast speed, it is nearly impossible to feel anything, let alone experience.

It's almost as if the feeling sensations get short-circuited by your brain's quick thinking (a.k.a. fast-mental processing). To feel something, you have to be present to it. Imagine holding a baby in your arms and feeling an outpouring of love. You were able to "register" these feelings of love (toward the baby) because you were "present" to the experience of love. You weren't thinking about your work or your grocery list or your next business meeting. Your attention was only on the baby, hence came the love at its strongest.

Similarly, when you start journaling about your daily life and your day-to-day emotions, you start to become present to them. You start to "register" your feelings and you become clear on how you really feel about certain things/situations/people/interactions in your life. There is no running away from uncomfortable situations anymore because you get to see your thoughts in black and white, on paper.

As an example, if, day in and day out, you journal that you are unhappy with your job, then chances are that by the end of 30 days, you will no longer evade the truth that you are miserable at your job. Then, you will most likely take appropriate actions to find a new one.

As your feelings become grounded, you finally begin to listen to the messages that your body is always sending you. You start to acknowledge what you feel at a much deeper level, and you honor those feelings. The thing is, the more you honor your feelings, the more frequent and persistent they become.

To make journaling even more effective, make sure that the content you write is for your eyes only. And make sure you do not edit your writing. In other words, write down exactly how you think, what you think, word for word. If you are angry with your friend, then write precisely that! Don't make it sound anything other than what it is.

You might have heard the phrase, **"If you can feel it, you can heal it."**

The simple act of writing down your thoughts, emotions, and charged memories will give you an opportunity to feel and discover yourself at a deeper, intimate level.

Over time, the charged memories start to lose their charge because, at some level, you make peace with your emotions. You no longer fight them, and you accept them for what they are.

You learn to forgive yourself and other people. This, in turn, changes your brain's chemistry and your emotional responses to your emotional triggers.

Tool #2: Resetting the Default Emotional Responses Through Meditation

We explored meditation in the section on the Mental Body Reset. In this section, we will explore how meditation can help you in resetting your default emotional responses.

Meditation can help you to detach from your emotionally charged memories, as well as emotional triggers.

Emotionally charged memories are extremely traumatic memories that keep a long-term grip on your mind. They can produce fear, anxiety, guilt, pain, even sorrow. These emotionally charged memories could be formed as a result of individual or collective events.

- Events such as 9/11, Hurricane Katrina, the Fukushima Tsunami, and the Gulf War cause emotional charge in the collective consciousness. The majority of people will probably remember where they were on 9/11, but will probably not know where they were on 9/10.

- Individual events such as any form of mental, physical, or emotional abuse can create an indelible mark in the psyche of a person.

Emotionally charged memories are usually suppressed by your subconscious, unless something in your environment triggers them to surface. The best way of dealing with emotionally charged memories is to find the suppressed memories and bring them into your consciousness. You must be willing to shine a light and look at seemingly dark places of your psyche. Your willingness alone is the first step in healing.

An emotional trigger is when someone or something sets you off, and your emotions get triggered. For example, say a friend of yours jokingly makes a mean comment about you, in front of your colleagues. While the comment may not be a big deal to another person, it totally destabilizes you.

You respond back with a knee-jerk reaction like anger or hostility, or you simply shut down emotionally. Reflecting on the situation later, you may realize how disproportionate your response was, and how out-of-place your reaction might have appeared.

You may get triggered by:
- Certain words, people, geographical locations, or environmental situations that provoke an excessive emotional response within you.
- A specific smell, physical feel, or taste that reminds you of the previous traumatic experience.

A few years back, when I was planning my first trip to Europe, I intuitively tuned into each country to get a feel for whether to visit it or not. When it came to Germany, I felt a sense of dread and sadness that knew no bounds. I knew that I was emotionally triggered, and so I let myself be and chose to not visit Germany on my first trip.

To detach yourself from emotionally charged memories and emotional triggers, you must be willing to look at the emotionally charged situations, no matter how uncomfortable they make you feel. You can't afford to sweep those charged emotions under the rug and pretend that the trauma never occurred. Your willingness alone is half the work. Knowing when you are emotionally triggered can save you from going into the downward spiral of agony and distress.

Meditation is an excellent tool for emotional healing for the following reasons.

Number one: it relaxes the Physical Body. This is important because:

- When you are emotionally triggered, your emotions tend to run high, your logical reasoning goes out the window, and your body goes into the fight-or-flight mode. Meditation relaxes the parasympathetic nervous system in such a way that the Physical Body is no longer in the fight-or-flight mode.
- It connects you with your breath, which automatically allows you to step out of your intellectual mind and into your body. This process can help detach you from the emotionally charged situation.
- At a physical level, there are many known benefits of meditation, such as mood elevation by releasing endorphins (hormones of happiness), improved sleep, lower stress, and a relaxed parasympathetic nervous system, among others.

Number two: meditation helps you in cultivating mindfulness.

- When you are present to your emotional pain and suffering, you can look at your challenging experiences from the standpoint of a neutral observer or a compassionate witness. When you give compassion to yourself, you stop the endless judgment of your emotional entanglements and give your Mental Body much-needed rest.

- When you are present, you can forgive yourself and others for the situations that, at one time, triggered you.

- In the present moment, you are not thinking about the past or the future. Your awareness is only in the "current" moment; it is in that moment where you can detach yourself from the emotional storms of the unhealed traumas, even if only temporarily.

As you develop a daily habit of meditation and mindfulness, the untamed emotions eventually soothe themselves into balance.

Number three: meditation relaxes the Mental Body.

- Meditation gently moves the neuron activity in your brain from a Beta (overstimulated) to an Alpha (calm) state. When you are in the Alpha state, you are privy to insights—information that is inaccessible in the Beta state.

- In the state of meditation, as an example, you may become aware of the real motives of other people, and you might become present to the underlying causes of situations and events that emotionally trigger you.

- You might become present to why you attracted certain traumatic experiences in your life and what you need to learn from these experiences.

Number four: meditation teaches discernment* instead of judgment.

This is very important because:

- Judgment and blame are the by-products of ego. Judgment is the mental ability to understand something, form an opinion, and reach a decision.

- In contrast, discernment is the personal resonance of people, events, and circumstances that you chose to engage with, based on whether they were aligned with you in the given moment or not.

- In simple words, discernment means determining what you choose to engage with, against your heart's desires. Unlike judgment, it is not ego driven; it has a heart resonance. As an example, it was my inner discernment that guided me to skip visiting Germany on my first trip to Europe.

- The answer on whether to engage with something or not can change from time to time, depending on when you ask the question and what powers of discernment you have cultivated.

- Learning personal discernment builds necessary boundaries to help you discover what is supportive and productive for you.

- Detaching yourself from emotionally charged experiences doesn't happen in the blink of an eye. It takes commitment and an earnest desire to free yourself from soul-sucking, mind-bending emotional storms and entanglements.

And that's where **creating a habit of daily meditation is worth its weight in gold**. Choose a meditation practice that works for you and **stick to it**.

You will know if your meditation practice is bearing fruit if you consistently find yourself at peace with yourself and others. You might even become somewhat detached from life and everything that happens around you. If this doesn't occur after a few months, try out different meditation technique and see if that makes any difference.

It wasn't until I started practicing meditation that I became present to my emotions at an intimate level. I clearly saw how I had reacted to my fear-based emotions in my life. Through developing a consistent meditation practice, I was able to get a handle on my emotional triggers and soothe my untamed emotions.

Nowadays, when an emotionally-charged situation comes up, I am less likely to feel overwhelmed or go into a tizzy. I can disengage myself from situations and people with much more ease than ever before.

While meditation is no magic potion, it just might be the closest thing to it.

*Source: www.energeticsynthesis.com

Tool #3: Developing Emotional Resilience

Emotional resilience is the ability to adapt to life's ups and downs and to sail through stressful situations.

Most over-analyzers use willpower, force, and determination to tide through life's challenges. The ability to "suck it up" and act as if everything is normal is quite common among them. In fact, for the longest time, this was exactly how I handled challenges in my life.

When you have no concept of feelings or their impact on you, then sucking it up seems the only choice available on the table. I remember my friends would tell me, "Let your emotions flow, let them wash over." I used to look at them with wide eyes and wonder, thinking to myself, "What the heck are they talking about?" As an intellectual, I was never able to make sense of what emotional resilience meant.

I was afraid that I might feel pain and discomfort while unraveling my suppressed emotions, and so, I avoided my feelings for as long as I could. This continued until I made a commitment to know all aspects of myself and vowed to accept myself with all my imperfections.

To cultivate emotional resilience, you will need to make peace with all your emotions—the good, the bad, the ugly, and everything in-between. Journal about your emotions, sing about them, write a poem, or speak to the universe about your emotions. The point is not to bottle up the feelings, whatever they may be. Get to know your feelings, and explore them with a child-like curiosity, without judgment or fear.

You have got to allow yourself to feel ALL of your emotions.

Emotions are not something you can think your way through. You must allow them to move through your body of their own accord. If you are someone who has bottled up your feelings for years, or perhaps even decades, know that it's never too late to give yourself permission to heal, to give yourself permission to let go of the emotional baggage that you have been carrying for all those years.

Change is a result of atomic-sized actions, taken every day. The more you allow yourself to feel, the easier emotional healing becomes.

As a side note, please be kind to yourself and other people in your life as you delve into your feelings and emotional states. If your feelings seem too intense, excuse yourself from your friends and family (if you can) and give yourself free space to be with yourself. Nurture yourself and just be.

Emotions are such an intrinsic part of the human experience that I don't think you can ever be "done" with experiencing challenging emotions. However, the more you work with your emotions, the easier they become to process.

When you start with your emotional healing, don't go looking for the end date of the process. It doesn't work that way. Make a commitment to heal, and then trust that your wounds will heal in the divine right order and timing. When you start managing your challenging emotional states with relative ease, you will know that you are on your way to developing emotional resilience and emotional intelligence. Trust yourself and trust the universe.

Vulnerability

One of the cornerstones of emotional healing is the ability to embrace vulnerability.

In 2012, I came across Brene Brown's famous TED Talk "The Power of Vulnerability," and it had a profound impact on me. As someone who was highly analytical in my approach to life, I always thought of vulnerability as a weakness. Women who overthink also view vulnerability as a weakness.

According to Brene Brown's book, this is what vulnerability looks like:
- "Not sucking it in anymore."
- "Sweaty palms and a racing heart."
- "Taking off a straitjacket."
- "It's where courage and fear meet."
- "Taking the first step to what you fear the most."

- "The terrifying point on a rollercoaster when you're about to tip over the edge and take the plunge."
- "It feels so awkward and scary, but it makes me feel human and alive."

The interesting thing is:

- You won't be an overthinker if you are willing to take off your straitjacket.
- You won't be an overthinker if you can let go of your need for perfectionism.
- You won't be an overthinker if you can embrace your fears and let your imperfections be seen.

You get the point, right?

Vulnerability often feels uncomfortable because you can never predict or control the outcome of a situation.

You may run away from vulnerability because you don't want to get hurt. It might feel easier and more manageable to overanalyze, than to deal with feelings of discomfort, rejection, hurt, or sadness.

As I started embracing vulnerability in my daily interactions, I realized most of the time I didn't speak my truth. I said things that others wanted to hear. I didn't want to ruffle any feathers, and I wanted to play the part of a nice person. Realizing my foolishness was a rude awakening. Slowly, I made course corrections and learned to speak my truth with everyone in my life.

Vulnerability heals the deep-seated disconnect between your head and your heart. When you embrace vulnerability, you get a new lease of life on all your relationships.

To connect with
our soul broadcast,
we have to
open our heart center &
be willing to allow feelings, & emotions.

If we block emotions,
we shut down our heart &
shut down
our soul communication.

Tool #4: Building a Support Tribe

Emotional work is personal and profoundly intimate. It takes courage, commitment, self-compassion, and a willingness to unravel and observe your default emotional responses. It always helps to have a support tribe to lean on when you start working with your Emotional Body.

Emotional healing occurs in waves and often it can feel like peeling the layers of an onion. It takes practice to change your default emotional responses and release the old emotional triggers.

The path to emotional healing is anything but a straight line. Sometimes the journey may take you down the narrow winding roads that lead to nowhere. While you will travel much of the path alone, it always helps to have a friend, a companion who is also vested in your growth, and who can hold the space for you.

Your support tribe is the group of people who will hold your hand and be there for you in times of emotional distress. It always helps to have the support of a close group of friends and/or family members.

Have at least two to three people with whom you can be emotionally honest and transparent. Ideally, someone who has done emotional healing of their own and can gently nudge you in the right direction when it gets challenging.

Surround yourself with people with whom you feel safe and can be vulnerable.

The thing is that no one can tell you what you must or must not do for your emotional healing. You may be offered tools and suggestions but, ultimately, you will have to test them against your own resonance and discern which of them work for you and which ones don't.

I was blessed to be surrounded by friends who had done a lot of emotional work. They could tell from a distance what I was working through and what I needed to do in order to resolve my emotional encumbrances. Over time, I learned the ropes of emotional work and was able to self-source the cause of emotional pain and what I needed to do to address the core issues.

Choosing Your Emotional Support Tribe

While you can choose to enroll as many people as you wish in your support tribe, make sure each person you choose has a modicum of emotional clarity and can hold compassion for you.

Look for people who demonstrate the following abilities:
- Someone with whom you feel emotionally safe.
- Someone who models emotional clarity and emotional resilience in their day-to-day interactions.

- Someone who offers kindness and patience in your life; these will be crucial as you maneuver through difficult emotional situations.
- Someone who is available and accessible to you when you need their intervention or guidance.

This group of people could include your friends, family, therapists, or acquaintances. Again, there is no right or wrong way to choose your support tribe. I always look for qualities of mutual respect and trust, besides the ones listed above, when I choose people to be a part of my emotional support system.

Family as the Support Tribe

Just because someone is your family does not qualify them to be a part of your support tribe. Why? Because they may not be emotionally available. Many times, family members are not able to meet the emotional needs of their loved ones.

So, while it's great to have the support of your family members (if they are emotionally resilient), make sure to include other people in your tribe.

The same argument also goes for your spouse. That is, just because someone is your spouse, it doesn't automatically mean they will have the emotional clarity to be a part of your emotional support tribe.

Tell Your Tribe How You Want to Be Supported

In the initial stages of emotional work, there might be times when you fall off the bandwagon. That is quite normal and, in some cases, almost certain. Remember when I shared with you that the path to emotional healing is not a straight line?

Through my own experiences, I have come to realize that there are bound to be times when you feel down and overwhelmed. During these times, you will need to ask for support.

When you're only starting out with your emotional work, your skills in emotional resilience might feel wobbly. Ask your friends and your emotional support tribe to rally around you at that time.

- Schedule regular check-ins with your friends. This could be a phone call or an in-person catch-up; whichever works best with you and your friend's schedule.
- Let your friends know how you want to be supported when feeling down. Do you want your friends to use certain words or phrases or stories to cheer you up? If so, let them know.
- Do you have a love language? Do you have a support language? Make sure you share it with your support tribe.

Tell your friends very clearly what they need to say to you when you're down and in need of support.

Can you think of three people that you can reach out to today and ask for emotional support? Name them here:

1. _____

2. _____

3. _____

Then see to it that you reach out to them.

Tool #5: Practicing Gentleness and Neutrality

I remember, for the longest time, my friends would say to me, "You are so hard on yourself," and I could never understand what they meant by that. My mind was always striving for the next goal and the next prize. I used to live by a timetable and devote every hour to one specific activity. I could not imagine the thought of doing nothing. In fact, I always thought that relaxing was such a waste of time.

Well, that's the beauty of the analytical mind. It wants to explore a million things; unfortunately, it wants to do them all at once.

Always being on the go can be a great asset when completing the last leg of a project, or to get the work done in a time crunch. However, as a lifestyle choice, it can have a detrimental effect.

Most women who overthink and overanalyze have a strong inner critic. I often found it challenging to be gentle with myself. It took me a long time to realize that being gentle with myself could be a great emotional asset to have and draw upon.

You can't be gentle with other people unless you are gentle with yourself.

They say that charity begins at home. The next time your mind wants to lash out at you because you couldn't get something right or perfect, pause there for a moment. And ask yourself, "Would I ever treat my beloved or a loved one the way I am going to treat myself right now?" And if your answer is no, then it's time for you to direct a shining beacon of compassion and love toward yourself.

There is no magic potion that I can share with you that will instantly turn you into a self-loving person. Trust me, if I had one, I would share it with every single person on this planet.

You must remind yourself (sometimes, repeatedly), that self-love and gentleness is the <u>only way</u> to develop emotional resilience.

I know it's not fun having to remind yourself continually that you have got to be kind to yourself. It took me a while to realize that being gentle toward oneself is a sign of great strength and emotional maturity.

Since I started embracing and embodying self-love, I have noticed a stark shift in my attitude toward my friends and family. Where before I would get triggered by the slightest of things, now I am much kinder and gentler about things being imperfect.

And if I must critique myself or others, then I do so with infinite gentleness.

Choosing Neutrality

Highly analytical women tend to see things in extreme polarities, such as good or bad, negative or positive, black or white, while forgetting that there is always a middle ground (a point of neutrality) to choose from. When you are neutral, you no longer carry charge about any situation, person, place, or thing, and you are no longer swinging in the extremes. You don't have an agenda or moral uprightness about situations.

The journey from extreme emotional polarities to finding a middle ground, the point zero, is at the heart of becoming emotionally centered and neutral.

Consider a scenario where you have had a huge fight with your best friend or your partner. Your thoughts might be swirling around about how unfair your friend or partner is and how great it would be if only they could see your point of view. Let's say you feel hurt, not heard, or you feel invisible in your relationship. What do you do then?

Do you go on a rant and call everyone in your friend circle to tell them how unfair your friend or partner is? Or do you let things be until you feel neutral about this fight?

Whenever I find myself in emotionally sticky situations, like a fight or an argument with a friend, I always ask to be divinely guided to neutrality.

In some cases, choosing neutrality comes easy, while in others, it is next to impossible.

However, the more you remind yourself to choose neutrality on a day-to-day basis, the easier it becomes to stay neutral in sticky situations. Learning to hold neutrality can be your biggest asset in many emotionally challenging circumstances. Choosing neutrality is a lifesaving tool that is worth developing.

The power of choice is always yours. When your emotions run high (and I assure they will from time to time), find ways to bring neutrality in your thoughts and actions.

Tool #6: Learning to Nurture the Inner Self

Learning to nurture yourself is the cornerstone of self-care and self-love. As an over-analytical person, I used to think of self-nurturing as entirely unnecessary and, to be honest, obsessive.

I couldn't have been more wrong!

An online dictionary defines nurture as:
- The action of raising or caring for an offspring.
- The fostering or overseeing the development of something.
- To raise or educate.
- To provide sustenance for (to nourish).

So, by definition, self-nurture would mean that all these traits were directed toward yourself. Are you still with me? For an overthinking mind, self-nurture is the ability to take care of yourself not just mentally or physically, but also emotionally. It is a vital part of the Emotional Body Reset.

Self-nurture is the pre-requisite for emotional healing.

A large percentage of women (regardless of whether they overthink or not) tend to put themselves at the bottom of their priority list. They will usually nurture everyone in their life except themselves. I know I used to do that, and I used to get very angry when my friends wouldn't nurture me back.

Wayne Dyer says that "***We can only give away to others what we have inside ourselves.***" In the context of self-nurture, it means that you can't nurture and help others unless you nurture yourself first. Learning to love yourself and to be gentle and kind towards yourself is an invaluable lesson that makes emotional healing infinitely smoother.

When you learn to work with your Emotional Body, there can be times when your emotions feel extremely raw, or you may feel emotionally exposed. During these emotionally stressful times, knowing how to nurture yourself can make all the difference in how you respond to these situations in your life.

The first step toward self-nurture starts with making a list of all the activities that fill your heart with joy. It could be something as simple as buying yourself fresh flowers, getting a massage, getting your hair blowout, making yourself a cup of hot tea, going out to your favorite coffee shop, or doing some painting, sculpting, exercising, or hand-writing letters to yourself or your friends.

Make a list of activities that make you feel grounded in your body and fill your heart with joy.

Find an activity that works for you and that you can enjoy on your own. It might take several attempts before you narrow down to one or two activities that make your heart sing and make you completely come alive.

Through many attempts, I have noticed that nothing recharges and nurtures me like yoga. No matter how awful my mood is, a good yoga class never fails to cheer me up. I always step out of a yoga class feeling calm, centered, and at peace. My second favorite self-nurture activity is to spend time at my favorite café. Both activities can be done on my own and require no more than 30 minutes to an hour.

I have a giant poster in my apartment with "Yoga" written on it. It's my cue for what to do when things become overwhelming. I also tell all my friends that if they ever find me feeling depressed or drowned in emotional distress, then they must remind me to go to a yoga class.

Now, your turn. Can you think of at least two activities that bring you joy? List them here:

1. _____

2. _____

I recently came across a poem by Kamal Ravikanth that left an indelible mark in my mind. It reminds me to nurture myself, to always be kind and gentle to myself.

"When you like a rose,

You pluck it.

When you love a rose,

You water it.

You,

I want to water daily."

Section 4: Removing Fear From the Physical Body

Chapter 8 — Your Body's Reaction to Fear

We discussed in Chapter 1 that fear responses exist in all four layers of the human body—Mental, Emotional, Physical, and Spiritual. In this chapter, we will explore the fear responses triggered by the Physical Body.

We will start by discussing what fear physically feels in your body. The next time you feel fear, take a moment to observe what's happening with your body.

- Is fear making your heart beat faster?
- Do you feel anxious about what will happen next?
- Do you feel sweat trickling down your forehead?
- Did your mind shut down?

Really pay attention to what's happening inside your body.

We all have unique responses to fear in our body. Perhaps you are someone who has a mild fear response in your body, and so, for you, fear feels just like a mild discomfort. Or perhaps you are someone who feels fear, possibly other emotions as well, very intensely and can relate to all the symptoms above.

There is no right or wrong way of what a fear response should be; you simply need to be aware of how it manifests in your body.

As an example, when I feel fear in the Physical Body, my mind blanks out. I am physically in one place, and mentally in another. My mind is spitting out all the worst case, what-if scenarios. My appetite diminishes, and all I want to do is go back into my shell and avoid everyone.

Knowing how fear feels in your body is integral to the Physical Body Reset.

You might wonder why knowing the fear responses in your Physical Body matter. Here are the top two reasons:
- When you see something for what it is, it starts to loosen its charge on you. When you know how fear feels in your body, you have a choice to no longer operate from your impulsive reactions.
- The more you develop self-awareness, the easier it becomes to let go of things. Identifying your fear responses makes you less prone to extreme emotions because a part of you is able to clearly see when you are experiencing a "full-on" fear response.

The majority of the work in overcoming fear and failure and in resetting the Mental, Emotional, and Physical Bodies is to pay attention to what's going at the mental, emotional, and physical level.

Once you know how fear shows up in your body, you can make empowered choices such as:

-   Walking away from situations, people, and events that trigger your fear responses.
-   Grounding your Physical Body when you are triggered by fear.
-   Breathing deeply until the fear responses are gone.

When your body is in a state of fear, your first goal should be to find a way to center yourself, and to come back to neutrality and stillness.

Chapter 9 — Your Brain on Fear

An integral part of the Physical Body Reset is to alter the fear responses (such as anxiety, panic, unease, etc.) in your body. When you know how your body responds to fear, you can stay present (in situations) instead of reverting into your default ways of responding. This enables you to make new choices in how you respond in the face of fear.

In this chapter we will talk about:

- Areas of the brain where fear originates from.
- Conditions that cause the body to go into fight-or-flight mode.
- Common emotional states associated with fear.
- And, most importantly, why we get stuck in fight-or-flight.

The Three-Parted Brain Model

According to the triune brain model, human behavior is influenced by three major clusters of brain structures: the neocortex, the limbic brain, and the reptilian brain.

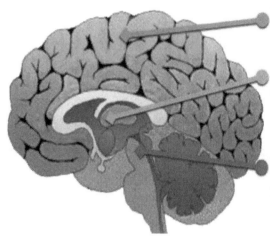

Neocortex:
Rational or Thinking Brain

Limbic Brain:
Emotional or Feeling Brain

Reptilian Brain:
Instinctual or Dinosaur Brain

The **neocortex** is the conscious, analytical, and logical brain. This is the part of your brain you use to operate in the 3D world.

The **limbic brain** is also called the middle brain. Like the neocortex, it is a conscious and rational brain. This is the part that makes you feel your emotions. Love, anger, rage, jealousy, and the whole myriad of emotions come from this part of your brain.

The **reptilian brain** is also known as the **survival brain**. It is the unconscious (subconscious, if you will) brain. This is the part of the brain that takes your hand off the hot stove. It is incredibly fast at responding to external stimuli to keep your Physical Body safe.

Of these three brain structures, two are conscious (the neocortex and midbrain) and one is unconscious (the survival brain). *The unconscious part of the brain, called the reptilian brain or the survival brain, is what kicks in when you feel fear.* Let's find out how this survival brain works and how it affects your entire being.

Survival Programs in the Brain Software

The lower brain (reptilian brain) runs in three modes: relaxed, fight/flight, and freeze. Using a traffic light as a model (according to the polyvagal theory), we see the three modes as follows:

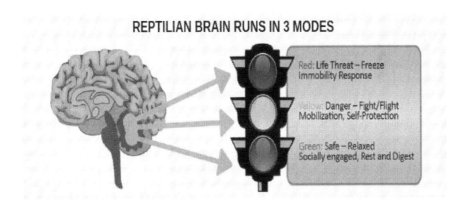

REPTILIAN BRAIN RUNS IN 3 MODES

Red: Life Threat – Freeze
Immobility Response

Yellow: Danger – Fight/Flight
Mobilization, Self-Protection

Green: Safe – Relaxed
Socially engaged, Rest and Digest

The **relaxed state** is like a green traffic light. In this state, your body is relaxed, and your heart and respiration are slow; you can digest your food, you can take a nap, you can enjoy being with loved ones, and you can relate to them.

The **fight/flight state** is like the yellow traffic light. In this state, the brain feels there is a looming danger, which leads to the fight/flight mode. *Your body was designed to stay in the fight/flight mode for extremely brief periods of time*. In the yellow zone, your body cannot digest food, you cannot sleep soundly, and you cannot enjoy or relate to your loved ones.

The **freeze zone** is like the red traffic light. This is where the lower brain perceives that the body is not going to survive an experience and shuts it down. The body becomes immobilized and is anesthetized to minimize suffering, and the body becomes dead. This happens in a split second.

The Fight/Flight State (a.k.a. Yellow Zone) of the Reptilian Brain

The danger zone of the survival brain is the yellow light (the fight/flight state), sandwiched between the relaxed state and the dead/frozen state. This zone of the brain "turns on" whenever there is imminent danger perceived by your brain.

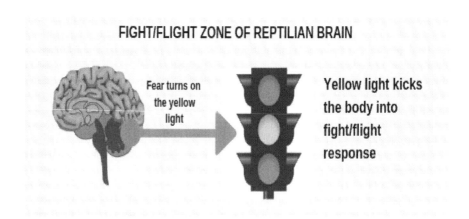

FIGHT/FLIGHT ZONE OF REPTILIAN BRAIN

Fear turns on the yellow light

Yellow light kicks the body into fight/flight response

Whenever your mind perceives any fear, your body kicks in the fight-or-flight response (that is, yellow traffic light of the reptilian brain).

The fight/flight response means that the vagus nerve (the nerve responsible for instinctive responses in the body) shuts down all the organs below the diaphragm and speeds up those above the diaphragm. You get an immediate increase of available energy, sometimes superhuman strength, in order to escape danger. This is an amazing thing that your body can do in a split second.

The Reptilian (Survival) Brain and Its Emotional States

When the reptilian (survival) brain is in the yellow zone, there are several emotions that can manifest in the body. These emotions include panic, anxiety, unease, rage, anger, and irritability.

EMOTIONAL STATES OF REPTILIAN BRAIN

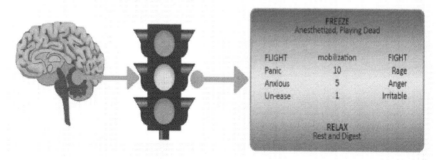

Do you identify with any of the emotional states from the image above?

Do you know your default state of being? Your default state is the emotional state that you find yourself in constantly (especially when there is no perceived outside threat).

Is your default state being anxious? Or is it being angry?

I have a dear friend, Rose, whose default state is being anxious. Her anxiety is often visible in the way she carries herself, in her eyes, in her facial expressions, in the tone of her voice, and the way she reacts to mundane situations in her life. I always have to remind my friend to take deep breaths through the day and to learn to relax.

Based on the image above, you and I know that when my friend is feeling anxious, she is operating from the fight/flight mode (the yellow traffic light of the reptilian brain). This means she is not in a state to make decisions that involve critical thinking and analysis because the part of her brain responsible for making conscious choices is not available for mental processing when her body is in a state of anxiety.

Here are three key reasons why you can get stuck in a fight/flight state:
- You feel that you are in an unsafe situation and the accurate assessment is that you are in danger or your life is threatened. In this situation, your brain will remain in the fight/flight state until you get to a safe place.

- You might come across situations that you feel you have no control over. Again, your brain will treat this situation as a threat and remain in the fight/flight mode.
- You may have unresolved trauma from the past, and the current circumstances resemble the traumatic ones. Your brain perceives this situation as a real threat.

If your survival brain was designed without any technical glitches, then it would be safe to assume that in an ideal world, you would:
- Detect danger, at which point your survival brain would kick into the yellow zone (the fight/flight zone).
- This would give you a boost of energy for a short time.
- Your survival brain would then go back into the relaxed (green) state, once the perceived danger was gone.

However, you and I know that your survival brain does not work as elaborated in the steps above. Here's why.

When was the last time you were angry at someone? Like really, really angry? And how long did that anger last? A few minutes? A few hours? A few days? If you answered anything other than a few minutes, then we know that your survival brain went into the yellow zone and stayed there much longer than it was supposed to.

When you are stuck in the emotional state of the yellow traffic light, you now know that fear (or anger, or any other adrenaline-fueled emotion) is raging in your body. In order to shift gears of your brain from the yellow state to the green state, you will need to change how you are responding to these challenging situations in your life.

*Source: Adapted from www.energeticsnthesis.com

Chapter 10 — Tools for the Physical Body Reset

To remove the fear responses from your Physical Body, you will first need to embody it. When you expend excessive mental energy (as with overthinkers and overanalyzers), you tend to live in your head instead of your body. Overstimulated mental energy makes you a "balloon person"—a balloon head with a tiny string body.

You can't release fears from your Physical Body unless you first learn to embody it.

Let's talk about what it means to embody the Physical Body:

- Embodiment, in this context, means becoming more aware of how you feel in your body so that you "think" not only with your mind, but also with your body.

- You become consistent and coherent, both in your internal and external world because you feel deeply connected to the true aspect of yourself.
- You become aware that your body and mind function together in a harmonious partnership.

In the book "Path to Empowerment," Barbara Marciniak says that your physical body is wired with innate intelligence, and you must make it your business to learn to tap into this inner wisdom and innate intelligence. And how do you learn to tap into the wisdom of the body? By listening to your body's messages.

The beauty of embodying the Physical Body is that in the face of unknown situations, when you don't know which road to choose, or whether to go left or right, you can call upon your body's intelligence to assist. And how? You pay attention to the way your body feels. When you are in sync with your body, you will know how a "Yes" feels in your body, and you will know exactly how a "No" feels, helping you discern which path to choose.

Over the years, I have learned to pay attention to my body's messages and to trust them, even if they go against my mental analysis. I once went for a job interview that went well, but by the time I got home from the interview, I felt sick to my stomach. Every time I thought about that new work opportunity, I felt a sense of sadness and dread. A week later, to my relief and surprise, I was presented with the job offer.

I wanted to feel gratitude, excitement, and joy, but I only found feelings of dread, sadness, and anxiety. I thought to myself, "This doesn't feel right. How can I possibly accept an offer that makes my heart anxious and unsettled?"

I had no doubt in my mind that my body was communicating to me that the new job offer would not be a good fit for me. I listened to the inner guidance and refused the offer—in turn, possibly saving myself from inner torment and stress.

Learning to hear and trust the body's messages and intelligence didn't happen overnight for me. It took time to train my overinflated Mental Body to accept and honor the wisdom and innate intelligence of my Physical Body. I can now tap into my body's wisdom at will and know exactly what I need to do (and not do) in most situations. In retrospect, it too, was one of the best investments I ever made in myself.

In this chapter, we will explore following tools to help you embody your Physical Body fully and for tapping into your body's innate wisdom.
1. Shifting Gears From Thinking to Feeling.
2. Tuning Into the Intelligence of the Body
3. Developing Heart-Based Intelligence.
4. Engaging in Full Body Movement.
5. Learning to Read the Energy Signature.
6. Honing the Inner Bullshit Detector.

Tool #1: Shifting Gears From Thinking to Feeling

In my experience, the greatest challenge for an analytical person is to get out of their thinking mind and into their feeling mind. Your mind can be your greatest ally or your greatest enemy. When you tend to overthink, and obsess over situations, people, or anything else, you tend to block the organic flow of energy. Instead of paying attention to how you feel about things, you get locked in your own mind.

Women who overanalyze tend to intellectualize everything, and their beautiful mind is always putting analysis on everything they are doing or plan on doing in the future. To an astute outsider, this obsession with analysis mostly appears strange, or even comical.

Don't get me wrong. I love to analyze things. I believe it's a natural outcome of the analytical mind. However, the problem arises when you overidentify with your rational analysis. In other words, your rational analysis takes center stage in your life and everything pivots around it.

As an overthinker, you might overlook your feelings and your intuition, especially if the intuitive guidance is diametrically opposite to what your mental analysis has determined as accurate. In short, you trust your intellectual analysis more than you trust your gut feeling. This is the core issue with an overthinking and an overly analytical mind that must be addressed.

You need to heal the inherent disconnect between your thinking and your feelings.

One of the most rewarding journeys an overthinker can take is the journey from thinking to feeling. The first step in shifting gears from thinking to feeling is to train your mind to slow down its thought processes. When your mind is scattered and moving from one thought to another at lightning speed, it is almost impossible to register or pay attention to what you're feeling in your body.

In order to feel things, you need to quieten your mind.

- One of the most useful tools to slow down the mental chatter is to just be. Just observe your body and your breathing, and observe the inner tension if it exists in any part of your body. Just this awareness alone will start to calm your mind.
- Walking in nature is another tool to slow down your brain activity. And so are journaling and meditation, besides the other tools we discussed in Chapter 4.

You need a quiet mind (slow brainwave activity) to become present with the sensations in your Physical Body.

You start by asking yourself how you feel in your body.

- Is your body feeling relaxed, tense, or agitated?
- Is there a sense of calmness and tranquility in your body?
- Does your body feel at peace?

Does your body feel the same at home and at work, or is there any difference? What does your body feel when you are in the company of your friends and loved ones? What does your body feel when you are interacting with your co-workers? Do they all feel the same, or different? Can you discern the different emotional states in your body?

Your body communicates to you through your feelings.

In other words, feelings are the language of your body. When you learn to distinguish and discern your feelings, you start to learn the language of your body.

Blocks That Prevent You From Feeling Your Way Through Things

1. The Mental Body's "Have-to" List
2. Psychological Defense Mechanisms

Block #1: The Mental Body's "Have-to" List

The majority of women who overthink and overanalyze can attest to having a long list of have-to activities. Their minds have convinced them that if they perform six different activities, then they will be much further along in their overall progress. Whether those endeavors make any sense or not is a different story. The have-to list makes the overanalyzers feel secure and it provides them with a modicum of the control they desperately seek.

The best way to move away from the have-to list of the Mental Body is to contemplate things that you always *want* to do. Perhaps you always wanted to take music or dance lessons, but kept postponing it because your analytical mind always told you how difficult it would be?

Are there any activities that you have always wanted to do, but kept putting them off to an unknown time in the future?

My Have-to List	My Want-to List
-	-
-	-
-	-

If your have-to list is longer than your want-to list, chances are that your analytical mind has tricked you and your heart into subservience.

As you ponder over the listed you created above, you will notice that:
- Your have-to activities are primarily mind-based.
- Your want-to activities are primarily heart-based.

Can you think of at least one heart-based activity that you can start practicing today or this week?

Block #2: Identify Psychological Defense Mechanisms

It is fairly common for most overthinkers and overanalyzers to resort to various defense mechanisms that look like:

- Being passive/aggressive in social interactions.
- Over-achieving (to compensate for failures).
- Worrying (the need to control your environment).
- Over-indulging in food, alcohol, drugs, or sex.
- Fantasizing (to avoid reality by retreating into one's mind).

You might identify with one or more psychological defense mechanisms listed above.

When your mind resorts to these coping mechanisms, it is primarily to dislodge pain and discomfort. If you have never given yourself permission to feel your feelings—as in deeply feel your anger, sadness, pain, or even rejection—it can feel overwhelming to even think of acknowledging your feelings. I know I sure felt that way.

I often felt afraid to feel challenging emotions like anger and sadness. Whenever I felt a surge of sadness or fear, I would look to food for comfort. This continued until I found a way to work through the intense feelings in my journal.

"Out of your mind and into your body" should be the mantra for all overthinkers.

One of the best ways to overcome overthinking and overanalyzing is to learn to tap into the wisdom of your body. Granted, that it might take time and regular practice to register your feelings and emotions, but eventually, the process becomes second nature.

A word of caution. While it's one thing to learn how your emotions feel in your body, you obviously don't want to get stuck in your feelings. It's one thing to acknowledge and discern how anger feels in your body, and quite another to spend all day seething in anger or wallowing in self-pity. This is a common pitfall on the journey to emotional wellness, and I wanted to point it out for you.

Why Bother Feeling Your Emotions?

The foundation of the Physical Body Reset is built on your ability to feel your emotions in your body. Unless you are willing to acknowledge and register how your emotions feel in your body, you will not be able to tap into the innate wisdom and intelligence of your body.

When you feel your emotions, you give yourself an opportunity to heal them. As they say, "If you can feel it, you can heal it."

- When you become present to your emotions, you stop running away from them, and you can finally take responsibility to change them. As an example, you can't change sadness or anger unless you first acknowledge to yourself that you are sad or angry. The first step in healing is always recognizing that you are in pain and in need of an intervention.

- It is much easier (for an imposter spirit) to deceive your thought processes than to fool your body sensations or your emotions.
- Your body is like a finely tuned antenna, and its innate intelligence supersedes the intelligence of your intellectual mind. Who wouldn't want to access this innate power, right?
- Learning to feel your emotions will help you to heal the inherent disconnect between your mind and your body/heart.
- Learning to feel your emotions will help you to tune into the innate wisdom and intelligence of the body (more about this in the next tool).

I have often wondered that there must be a reason why our bodies are significantly larger than our brains. Perhaps they serve a bigger purpose that we haven't explored yet? It was a humbling experience for me to realize that my body knows much more than my analytical mind ever could. When you shift gears from thinking to feeling, you open yourself to a greater reality, one that you couldn't have accessed with your five senses alone.

Learning to discern how your body feels on a moment-to-moment basis is a powerful tool. As you start embracing your feelings, you will notice that:
- You trust your feelings as much as you trust your mental analysis.
- You honor your intuition as much as you honor your mental analysis.

Tool #2: Tuning Into the Intelligence of the Body

Human bodies are like sophisticated computers with a built-in intelligence of their own. Have you ever wondered why your heart keeps pumping blood without your slightest conscious awareness? The food you eat gets digested, assimilated, and excreted without any instructions from you. How does every cell in your body know when to multiply and when not to?

You can think of the intelligence of the body as your body's innate wisdom. Your body is always communicating with you through physical sensations, and, if you choose, you can learn to talk to your body.

Once you get comfortable with feeling your emotions, the next step is getting to know the sensation in your body.

Communicating With Your Body

A few years back, I took a class on body dynamics in Upstate New York. One of the things that the speaker talked about was becoming best friends with your body. She said that your body is coded with intelligence, and, if you choose, you can learn to communicate with it and tap into the wisdom of your body.

The speaker also suggested that, every single day after waking up, say to your body, "Body, body, body, I love you and I want to be friends with you. When you want to communicate with me, give me a gentle nudge or a gentle flutter and talk to me in signs that I can't miss."

This was such an alien concept to me, but I was intrigued beyond words. The analytical part of me just couldn't fathom if this could be real. I figured I had to give this a shot and see for myself if what the speaker had said was indeed true or not.

And so, for the next few months, every single morning upon waking up, I would say to my body, "Body, body, body, I love you and I want to be friends with you. When you want to communicate with me, give me a gentle nudge or gentle flutter and talk to me in signs that I can't miss."

I might have done this exercise for a few weeks, and much to my surprise (or rather, shock!), I started getting gentle nudges from my body. Faint whispers at first that slowly grew into a loud resounding voice. I started getting guidance on simple things, such as when to eat and when not to eat, when to go for exercise, and when to stay home.

The interesting thing is that these nudges were always spot on. As in: as long as I followed these nudges and the inner guidance, I would experience synchronicities in my days. Things would work out efficiently and effortlessly, and there would be a sense of ease and grace around my chores and work. And on the days I ignored the inner guidance, my days would be filled with chaos and frustration.

I was startled to experience this inner guidance from my body. I would wonder:

- How could my body know so much?
- How could my body know more than my analytical mind?
- How could my body know what was going to unfold in the immediate future?
- Was that even possible?

This was indeed a humbling experience for me.

When you connect with the intelligence of your body, it will feel like you are connecting with a good old friend who only has your best interests at heart.

If you are interested in accessing the intelligence of the body, set an intention that you want your body to guide you on a daily basis. It doesn't matter what words you choose, as long as you speak them with a heartfelt sincerity.

And when your body responds, follow that guidance. Your body can be your greatest ally, but only if you choose to develop a relationship with it.

Tool #3: Developing Heart-Based Intelligence

Your heart is one area of your body that communicates powerfully and extremely effectively with you. Have you noticed that in certain situations, your heart may skip a beat, get palpitations, flutter, or even feel as if it's going to burst open, depending on what is happening around you?

I am sure you have heard phrases like, "Follow your heart, it knows the way," or, "Your heart knows things that your mind cannot explain," or even, "Do what makes your heart come alive." The truth is that every cell in your body is intelligent, with your heart acting like a conductor, an overseer of the entire intelligence of the body.

When you connect with your heart, you align with a deeper source of intuitive intelligence that helps you to access the untapped potential within yourself.

The heart talks in its own language. Learning to talk with your heart can sometimes feel like learning a brand new language. The more you commit to communicating with your heart, the easier it will become to hear your heart's message.

Communicating With Your Heart

In my experience, one of the most effective tools for learning to communicate with your heart is journaling. In my own experience, after a few months of journaling, I got to a point where I could no longer write anything in my journal that wasn't aligned with my heart. When I attempted to write anything that didn't ring true in my heart, I would literally hear inside my head: "Cancel out what you just wrote. That is not how you feel in your heart."

Whenever I feel lost or confused about my choices or decisions, I always seek solace and guidance from my heart through journaling. I pay attention to what my heart is telling me. If, every single day, I get the same guidance, then I act upon it.

I can't even begin to tell you how many times I have put myself through situations that weren't completely aligned with my heart. And when things didn't work out, my heart would say, "Didn't I tell you so? When are you going to start trusting me?"

Through a series of making great and not-so-great decisions, I have come to realize that the best decisions are the ones that are aligned with my heart.

And how do you know if your decisions are aligned with your heart or not? Through your emotions. They will tell you.

You will notice that when you make a choice that is aligned with your heart, it will make you feel expansive, light-hearted, happy, at peace, or simply elated. You might even say to yourself, "This (decision) just feels right." You will no longer be stuck in the what-ifs. Your decisions will ring true to the core of your being.

Decisions aligned with your heart will always lead you to your highest evolutionary path, even if it doesn't appear so right away. There may be times that your heart guides you to make choices that your conscious mind would never make. Pay attention when that happens and follow the guidance of your heart.

Your heart is always talking to you, and the more you listen to its guidance, the louder its voice will get.

Tool #4: Engaging in Full Body Movement

Another excellent tool for Physical Body Reset is to engage in full body movement. Overthinkers and overanalyzers spend such an excessive amount of time thinking, analyzing, and strategizing that they can spend hours upon hours sitting in one place!

When you start to engage in full body movement, you become present to all the different parts of your body, and it becomes easier to ground yourself in your body.

There are many ways to engage in full body movement through activities such as yoga, tai-chi, qigong, Pilates, dancing, gardening, walking, etc.

Activities and exercises that slow down the breath are most beneficial for overthinkers.

A few years back, one of my meditation teachers suggested that I take up the study of yoga or qigong. She said it would give my busy mind a much-needed rest. I signed-up for both, yoga and qigong classes, and felt a natural inclination and resonance towards yoga. In retrospect, learning and practicing yoga was also one of the best gifts that I gave myself. Some of the most brilliant insights that I have ever received have come during the last asana of the yoga class, called "Savasana," where you lie down flat on your back after an extensive yoga session, and let go of your body and mind.

Choose one physical activity that you enjoy and commit yourself to practicing it at least a few times each week. I have noticed that sometimes I become so exceedingly engrossed in my work that I tend to think of exercise as a distraction. I couldn't be more wrong about that. In fact, those are precisely the times that I need it the most!

I have noticed that when I make time for yoga (even if only for 10 minutes), I am instantly refreshed and filled with new ideas and insights about my work; ideas and insights that I wouldn't have gotten any other way.

Tool #5: Learning to Read the Energy Signature

Have you ever experienced walking into a place of worship and feeling a deep sense of peace and calmness dawn upon you? It is as if you feel at peace simply by being in this place of worship.

The vibe of a person, thing, or a situation is its energy signature.

Usually, the first feeling or vibe that comes to your mind about a person, place, or situation is always spot on. Think of an energy signature as the "real intention" of a person. It is often the unspoken part of the conversation. The thing about energy signatures is that the only way to access them is through your feelings or intuition. As a woman, you are naturally blessed to be much more connected to your intuitive mind; you only need to trust your inner hunches.

Energy signatures can only be felt; you can't think your way into them.

Often women talk themselves out of how they truly feel about certain people, places, or situations—especially if their feelings are diametrically opposite to what their mind is telling them. It's human nature to rely upon thinking/analysis instead of intuition. And yet, when you start to trust your intuition (as much as you trust your thinking), you open a new door of possibilities that didn't exist before.

Think of the energy signature as a "resonance" or an "essence" of a person, place, or situation. It is relatively easy to trick your mind with sweet talk or false promises, but it is way harder to fool your emotions and the impact of your emotions on your body.

The energy signature is what you perceive beyond the glitz and glamour, beyond the sweet talk, beyond the facade, beyond all the hollow promises a person might make to your face. When a person says something, and the energy behind their words is the exact opposite, you should instantly know that you cannot trust such a person blindly.

You might wonder, what is the benefit of learning to read energy signatures?

For a start—energy doesn't lie.

Have you ever experienced meeting a person with whom you felt naturally relaxed? And then there are people with whom, no matter how hard you try, you always end up feeling uptight and contracted. You must have experienced this, haven't you?

That's an example of your feelings communicating the energy signature of the person. Pay attention when that happens.

When you are able to read energy signatures, you can discern (with your heart's resonance) which energies to engage with and which ones to ignore.

Can you imagine living a life where your core relationships and work situations intrinsically had a great vibe to them? How would your life look? Can you think of any actions to create this life?

One superb way to accomplish this is to pay attention to the energy signature of people, places, or situations that cross your path and to consciously choose situations that have an expansive energy signature.

Tool #6: Honing the Inner Bullshit Detector

This tool is an extension of Learning to Read the Energy Signature.

To develop your inner bullshit detector:

- Gauge the energy signature of a person, place, or situation.

- Determine where the energy signature lies on the detector.

- Act accordingly (decide if this is something worth engaging with or not).

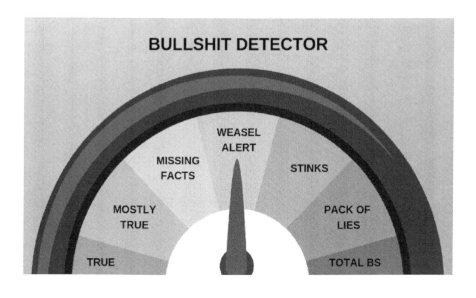

As you begin to hone your inner BS detector, there will be times when you falter, and you might wonder if you can trust your body's signals. That's absolutely normal and expected.

Would you expect to become an expert in biking on your first attempt? Probably not. Would you learn a new language overnight? Probably not.

Learning to read the energy signature is no different. It takes practice, commitment, and a fierce desire to want to develop a new skill.

Learning to read the energy signature of people, places, or situations around you is like tapping into an inner BS detector.

Let's consider a scenario. Say you're meeting a potential business partner who has had enormous success in running multiple businesses. Your potential partner looks perfect on paper. You meet this potential business partner, and let's assume he says all the right things to your face, but something about him feels off. You might think to yourself, "This person looks great on paper. Technically, there isn't any reason to not partner with him. But why am I not settled about this decision?"

What do you do in these situations?
- Do you listen to your head? Do you listen to your heart?
- Do you readily say yes to this new business partner because he said everything you wanted to hear?
- Or, do you sit on the proposal until your feelings are settled?
- How do you know if it's a real thing and not a con?

Personally, this is how I have come to hone the inner bullshit (BS) detector:
- When my feelings and thinking analysis are in sync, I think of it as a green light from the universe for projects and partnerships; in other words, it's Go time.

-   When my feelings and thinking analysis are not in sync, I think of it as a yellow light from the universe, meaning it's time to pause and wait until further information is given.

Through many painful mistakes, I have come to develop a deep reverence for what my feelings (or my body sensations) tell me.

I have come to realize that things work best for me when my thinking is in sync with what I am feeling in my body. And the more I listen to that inner guidance, the more refined my inner BS detector becomes.

Knowing whom to engage and whom to avoid can make all the difference between thriving and failing partnerships and relationships. This is where a high-precision inner BS detector can be worth its weight in gold.

Challenges on the Road to Honing Your BS Detector

The process I described for honing the inner BS detector is quite straightforward. Right? I mean, how difficult can it be to know how to act when your feelings and thoughts are in sync, and how to act when your feelings and thoughts don't align?

If only the world was as perfect as the statement above!

The thing is, when you have an analytical bent to your mind, there is almost an *over*-identification with what you *think* versus what you *feel*. You are so comfortable, so used to depending on your intellectual analysis, that when your feelings tell you anything different, you wonder how your feelings could know any better.

Well, my dear analytical friend, I have a news flash for you.

The intellectual mind is an infant, compared to the infinite wisdom contained in the intelligence of the human body. Think of the analytical mind as a drop in the ocean and the body intelligence as the ocean itself.

On a side note, never forget that it is much easier for any outside influence (imposter spirit) to fool your thoughts than to fool the feelings of your body.

HEALING ROADMAP

TOOLS FOR HEALING FEAR RESPONSES FROM THE MENTAL BODY

1. Affirmations
2. Daily Meditation
3. Meditation for Removing Core Fears
4. Journaling
5. Celebrating and Tracking Daily Failures
6. Phone Detox

TOOLS FOR HEALING FEAR RESPONSES FROM THE EMOTIONAL BODY

1. Exploring Emotions Through Journaling
2. Resetting the Default Emotional Responses Through Meditation
3. Developing Emotional Resilience
4. Building a Support Tribe
5. Practicing Gentleness and Neutrality
6. Learning to Nurture the Inner Self

TOOLS FOR HEALING FEAR RESPONSES FROM THE PHYSICAL BODY *BY LEARNING TO EMBODY THE PHYSICAL BODY*

1. Shifting Gears from Thinking to Feeling
2. Tuning Into the Intelligence of the Body
3. Developing Heart-Based Intelligence
4. Engaging in Full Body Movement
5. Learning to Read the Energy Signature
6. Honing the Inner Bullshit Detector

Section 5: Becoming an "Actionist" in the Face of Fear

Chapter 11 — Tools to Counter Potential Pitfalls

When you embark on a journey into the unknown, you will encounter many pitfalls along the way. In the face of fear and failure, you must always keep moving, and keep taking baby steps toward your goals, even when you don't have all the answers.

Emotional healing requires patience, effort, and commitment because you are re-educating yourself to think, feel, and live in more of an open, vulnerable, and honest way. This is the best investment I've made in myself. Hopefully, you will feel the same.

One of the best ways to safeguard yourself against fear is to choose projects aligned with your value system. When you do so, you automatically stay connected with your heart and don't get swayed easily by your fears of failing. I recommend this to all my overly analytical friends.

Learning the Art of Surrender

I wrote about learning to surrender in the section on healing the Mental Body, and I believe it will serve well to revisit it again. Learning to surrender was one of the hardest lessons I had to learn as an obsessively analytical person.

Most women who obsess over situations, people, or anything else also find it challenging to surrender. Perhaps you can surrender in the area of your health and career, but not when it comes to your children or your finances?

Just as you can't selectively numb emotions, you can't choose areas of your lives where you will surrender.

I always used to think of surrender as giving up. And I used to wonder, why in the world would anyone ever want to give up? Aren't we always taught, from the day we are born, to "Never, ever, give up and to keep chasing after your goals and dreams with all of your heart and mind?"

Imagine working day in and day out on a dream that you are absolutely passionate about (it could be your first business, your first love, your first big gig, or your first house); for a moment, imagine that your project tanks.

What do you do then?

Situations like these have happened to me all the time. And these situations always left me confused and in "fighting" mode. After all, how could I give up on my treasured projects? Right?

It wasn't until I started tapping into the energy of situations, people, and places that things finally began to shift for me. *Instead of being stuck with how I wanted "things" to be or people to act in my outer world, for the first time in my life, I observed the "energetics of things" as they were*. Meaning: I observed how situations in my life were evolving, rather than forcing them or dwelling upon them, wishing they were different.

I started making decisions, but not as a reaction to my ego. Rather, the decisions were based on where the energy was naturally flowing and moving. Instead of being afraid of how situations would pan out, I chose to trust the flow of the energy.

I felt as if I had finally learned to surrender.

Ultimately, I understood and experienced that surrendering meant tapping into the flow of the universe and paying attention to where the tides of the ocean take you.

At its highest level, surrender means that your faith and trust in the power of the Divine mind (or a God) supersede your fragile human mind. It means that you intrinsically trust that through the ebbs and flow of your life's journey, your Divine essence or God will bring you to the tranquil shores your soul has always yearned for.

You only need to be flexible so that the cosmic intelligence can work through you and your life.

When you soften your mind, like your heart, you truly open yourself to a world of new possibilities, new adventures, and explorations.

As you approach the end of this book, I want to thank you for being on this journey with me. Thank you for your generous time. I hope you have enjoyed reading this book and exploring tools for your emotional, physical, and mental healing.

To your greatest unfoldment!

What's Possible When We Do the Inner Emotional Work

99.99% of the inner work involved in clearing fears entails emotional healing. You can't permanently alter your default thought patterns and beliefs when your heart is hurting from past emotional scars and wounds.

Band-Aid solutions to soothe the emotional pain rarely work.

You can never run away from your unresolved emotional pain because the pain sneaks out when you least expect it. Try as you may to avoid it, when this deep-seated emotional pain comes gushing out and hits you like a ton of bricks, and you are forced to address it, then you can no longer hide from it.

I hope you won't wait that long before you consciously begin your emotional work. Overcoming fear and failure doesn't mean that fears and failures will magically disappear from your life. That never happens. The thing is, whenever you step into the unknown, you can never predict how things will pan out. In some situations, fear and failure are inevitable and expected. And in other situations, failure is guaranteed.

However, when you do the emotional work, fear no longer holds a tight grip on you because you have addressed your emotional pain and triggers through consistent inner emotional work. You become like a giant tree with deep roots, that can weather winter storms and high summer heat with equal ease and grace.

You might fall down a thousand times on the path to overcoming your fears and failures; the trick is in always finding a way to rise and try again, to keep moving forward, only forward. I am reminded of the poem "Still I Rise" by Maya Angelou.

Still I Rise

You may write me down in history
With your bitter, twisted lies,
You may trod me in the very dirt
But still, like dust, I'll rise.

Does my sassiness upset you?
Why are you beset with gloom?
'Cause I walk like I've got oil wells
Pumping in my living room.

Just like moons and like suns,

With the certainty of tides,
Just like hopes springing high,
Still I'll rise.

Did you want to see me broken?
Bowed head and lowered eyes?
Shoulders falling down like teardrops,
Weakened by my soulful cries?

Does my haughtiness offend you?
Don't you take it awful hard
'Cause I laugh like I've got gold mines
Diggin' in my own backyard.

You may shoot me with your words,
You may cut me with your eyes,
You may kill me with your hatefulness,
But still, like air, I'll rise.

Does my sexiness upset you?
Does it come as a surprise?
That I dance like I've got diamonds
At the meeting of my thighs?

Out of the huts of history's shame
I rise
Up from a past that's rooted in pain
I rise
I'm a black ocean, leaping and wide,
Welling and swelling I bear in the tide.

Leaving behind nights of terror and fear
I rise
Into a daybreak that's wondrously clear
I rise
Bringing the gifts that my ancestors gave,
I am the dream and the hope of the slave.
I rise
I rise
I rise.

Acknowledgments

I want to thank my father for his unshakable belief in me. Thank you, Dad, for being my biggest champion. You are a quintessential role model of service, sincerity, and commitment in my life. You always give me strength and courage to pursue my goals and visions. Thank you for being you.

I want to thank my first meditation teachers, Ramtha and JZ, for teaching me that my thoughts create my reality and that I can achieve anything with unwavering focus. I also want to thank Barbara Marciniak for teaching me about the innate intelligence and wisdom of the Physical Body.

Thanks are due to another gifted teacher, Lisa Renee, for helping me understand the mind-body connection and educating me about the negative ego programs. Lisa, you are a shining beacon of integrity, kindness, and strength. Thank you for your work and service.

I want to express my sincere gratitude to my dearest friend Terri Fellows. Thank you for being an embodiment of emotional clarity, strength, and truth. Thank you for being my soundboard through all my emotional challenges. Terri, from you, I have learned to embrace all emotions without judgment.

Thanks are also due to my family members and all my friends for always supporting me through all of my endeavors.

Thank you, God, for helping me heal myself from the fear programs. Thank you for all the challenges; they made me the person I am today. Thank you for always nudging me to take the high road and giving me the courage to serve humanity.

Additional Resources

Book Recommendations:

- For Journaling
  - "The Artist's Way" by Julia Cameron
  - "Writing Down Your Soul" by Janet Conner and Jane Cramer
- For Honing Body Intelligence
  - "Path of Empowerment" by Barbara Marciniak
  - "Women's Bodies, Women's Wisdom" by Dr. Christiane Northrup
  - "Discovering the Body's Wisdom" by Mirka Knaster
- For Emotional Clearing and Healing
  - "The Gifts of Imperfection" by Brene Brown
  - "I thought it Was Me (But It Isn't)" by Brene Brown
  - "The Dance of Anger" by Harriett Lerner
  - "Emotional Freedom" by Dr. Judith Orloff
  - "Emotional Agility" by Susan David
  - "The Nice Girl Syndrome" by Beverly Engel
  - "The Four Levels of Healing" by Shakti Gawain
- Meditation
  - "The Book of Awakening" by Mark Nepo

- o "Autobiography of a Yogi" by Paramahansa Yogananda
- o "The Places That Scare You" by Pema Chodron
- Miscellaneous
  - o "The Crossroads of Should and Must" by Elle Luna
  - o "The Alchemist" by Paulo Coelho
  - o "The Prosperous Heart" by Julia Cameron
- Guided Meditations
  - o Energetic Synthesis at www.energeticsynthesis.com
  - o Brain Sync at www.brainsync.com

Bonus Material

Download a copy of a free mini workbook by clicking here:

http://eepurl.com/gimJRH

In this workbook, you will access . . .

- Journaling prompts to heal fear and failure programs.
- Five-minute meditations techniques to align the body, mind, and spirit.
- Identify common fear patterns holding you back.
- Three-step blueprint that helps you move into the unknown.
- Suggestions/prompts for embracing daily failure.
- Discover options to add joy and happiness into your lifestyle.
- Create a plan to move forward and jumpstart your new habits and life.
- And much more!

About Kiran Bedi

I am a researcher, explorer, and a creator at heart. I love connecting dots and seeing how everything fits together. I am passionate about all things related to health and wellness. Things related to spirituality, quantum mechanics and neuroscience make my soul come alive.

I grew up in India, in a family of teachers. My early life revolved around school and academia. At college, I pursued physics and graduated with a master's in science from SUNY Buffalo, New York. Upon graduation, I began working with some of the top investment banks and consulting companies in New York, Seattle, and California.

In 2008, I had a breakdown that led to an out-of-body experience. This transcendental experience forever changed the trajectory of my life. It felt as if one day, I woke up as a completely different person.

Over the next few years, I explored different types of meditation and fell in love with journaling, for it enabled me to examine the contents of my mind and helped me develop self-awareness. I became acutely aware of my thoughts, behaviors, attitudes, and my thinking patterns through a daily journaling practice.

Through self-discovery and self-awareness, I uncovered many deep-seated "limiting" belief systems. As I encountered my core fears, I also became present to the fear I felt in my body. The scientist in me became fascinated at my own responses to fear and failure, and the researcher in me vowed to heal the way I reacted to fear and failure.

It was a rollercoaster ride to learn the language of emotions. Observing my emotions and being aware of them was a great challenge for my overly analytical mind. I didn't realize how much I trusted my intellectual analysis over my gut feelings. The journey from head to heart was no mean feat for an overthinker like me.

Through the process, I became deeply aware of the blocks that prevent intellectuals from embodying their physical bodies and trusting their gut and heart messages.

As I started sharing my newly found insights on emotional healing with my friends and colleagues, most of them not only related to my stories, but also shared similar challenges. It surprised and shocked me to witness the similarities in our experiences. This book is a step forwards in helping overly analytical women stand in their power.

I am passionate about helping women, especially those who tend to overthink. I hope this book helps women overcome their fear and failure blocks, and helps them become the best version of themselves.

Made in the
USA
Middletown, DE